THE SUCCESSFUL TRADER
Building Wealth for Your Future
In Only 5 Minutes a Day

THE SUCCESSFUL TRADER: BUILDING WEALTH FOR YOUR FUTURE IN ONLY 5 MINUTES A DAY

Copyright © 2014 Jeremy Downing
Book Editing: Pam Pieroni
Back Cover Photography: Duncan Kerridge
Cover Design: Susan Veach
Interior Layout & Graphics: Zanna Jezek, Samantha Stewart

Limitation of Liability/Disclaimer of Warranty: While the author and publisher have used their best efforts in preparing the book, they make no representations or warranties with respect to the accuracy or completeness of the contents of this book and specifically disclaim any implied warranties for a particular purpose. It is sold on the understanding that the publisher is not engaged in rendering professional, financial or legal services and neither the publisher nor the author shall be liable for damages arising from herein. If professional advice or other expert assistance is required, the services of a competent professional should be sought. Any business that the reader may start as a result of reading this book is not guaranteed to make money.

Printed in the U.S.A.
10 9 8 7 6 5 4 3 2 1

Library of Congress Cataloging-in-Publication Data
Downing, Jeremy, 1966

THE SUCCESSFUL TRADER: BUILDING WEALTH FOR YOUR FUTURE IN ONLY 5 MINUTES A DAY

ISBN-13: 978-0-9916089-4-2
ISBN-10: 0991608941

Summary: A guide to building wealth for your future in only 5 minutes a day.
1. Business & Money 2. Trading 3. Options 4. Stocks 5. Retirement Planning 6. Investing

DistinctPress.com
6822 22nd Avenue N., Suite 345
Saint Petersburg, Florida 33710-3918

COMPLAINTS: At Distinct Press we realize that we are far from perfect, but we do try and do the impossible, which is to create a book that will bring the reader a perfect experience. If and when you find an error or omission in our book, please write to us first so we can make things right, and only giving us this chance, consider leaving a complaint on the Internet. We strive for excellence but we also rely on your feedback to keep us covered and at the top of our game. We so appreciate you, the reader, and we'll do what we can, as fast as we can, to make any corrections and repairs. Write to pleasefixit@distinctpress.com.

For more information visit: www.the-successful-trader.com

THE SUCCESSFUL TRADER

Building Wealth for Your Future
In Only 5 Minutes a Day

Jeremy Downing

A DISTINCT PRESS BOOK
U.S.A.

This book is for all those who come to realize that time,
above all things, is the most precious and scarce of all life's resources.
I wish for you, above all, true wealth: the perfect mixture of time,
for those you love and wish to help (both near and far), and the ability
to earn the resources that give you that free time.

It is also for my family, Deborah, Sam and Luke, without whom
I would not have reached the realization above. I love them more
than they will ever know and I thank them for the gift of
every day I spend with them.

CONTENTS

Acknowledgements

This book would not be possible without the help and support of many people. Thank you Karl, Amer, Wal, Simon, Ed, and Richard - *The Cashflow Trader Program* 'pioneers' who put faith in me and my abilities to lead them to trading success.

Thank you to all those who have encouraged me to step up and serve, you know who you are.

Thanks to all my mentors throughout the last 13 years. It has been a journey that has taken longer than I imagined, but I wouldn't have missed it for the world!

I've learned to enjoy the journey and realize that I don't want to stop!

Introduction

This book builds three central arguments:

1. Our current investment systems are broken. Relying on other people to secure wealth for your future is a system that is no longer trusted, but there is an alternative and the alternative is you.

2. You are the best person to look after your financial future. You are the one who cares most about it and so it makes perfect sense for you to take control of the wheel and drive yourself to that better destination.

3. Anyone, and that means you, can learn to trade. In fact, the 'person in the street' has more access to low risk solutions in trading than most fund managers.

This book consists of five parts.

Part One will take you personally through my journey of experiencing the five biggest obstacles to trading success.

These Obstacles are:

1) Our 'Buy and Hold' Mentality – Thinking We Can Only Make Money In One Direction
2) The Dangers Of Emotion – Fear and Greed
3) Misuse of Leverage
4) Over Complex Strategies
5) Not Having a Big Enough Reason Why

It will show you how you can overcome these obstacles and avoid them from day one.

Part Two will introduce you to the stock market and options trading. It will explain how most people use options in the market and why we are not going to do things that way. It will show you how to adopt a low risk approach into very safe option strategies. These strategies will create a monthly income for you from the stock market.

Part Three will show you how to develop the correct mindset for trading. In every field of life where you see success, the thing that was behind it all was having the correct mindset. That, followed closely by the correct preparation, and then the correct actions.

Part Four will show you how to manage your trading income so that you build true wealth over time. It will also give you a guided tour of the principles of compounding. It will show you what can be achieved using what Albert Einstein called 'the eighth wonder of the world'.

And finally, Part Five will show you how to get started and prepare you for your trading journey. Part Five also includes an online resource page you may access at any time:

www.The-Cashflow-Trader.com/BookBonus

The above website provides you with a trading toolkit of free resources to help you on your journey.

Trading, just like anything else in life, can be made complex or it can be made simple.

There is a whole industry and system out there that wants you to believe that it is complicated. The reality is that there are simple solutions to be found, used and enjoyed.

A long time ago a man called Tony Robbins told me something very important. Here is what he said. "If you're not getting the right answer in life, you are not asking yourself the right question." The reason most people don't find a simple trading solution and a simple way to build wealth is that they don't ask themselves the right question.

So before you start reading further, ask yourself, out loud, the following question:

> "How can I find a simple way to make a great return in just five minutes a day?"

It took me six years to ask myself that question. The answer to that question is in the pages of the book you are about to read.

Enjoy!

Jeremy

Jeremy Downing
Founder of *The Successful Trader*
Creator of *The Cashflow Trader Program* and
The Options Trading Master Class

PART ONE

Part One will take you through my journey of personally experiencing the five biggest obstacles to trading success. There is a chapter on each of the five obstacles.

1) The 'Buy and Hold' Mentality
2) Emotions
3) Leverage
4) Over Complex Strategies
5) Not having a Big Enough Reason 'Why?'

This section will show you how you can overcome these obstacles and avoid them from day one.

Chapter One – The 'Buy and Hold' Mentality

Our Current Investing Systems Are Broken

Yes, our current investing systems are broken. Not the stock market itself, but the way we have been taught to use it. Let's take a step back and take a long, cool, and hard look at what we have been taught to do.

From the time we were young, our parents or guardians told us to save, to put some of our money aside. "Save for a rainy day" they would tell us. "Don't spend all of your money at once." At face value, it is good advice and for a long time during our early developmental years, that strategy worked. We could trust the banks and most of us grew up with savings accounts, which showed us the benefits of saving by providing healthy interest rates. As we grew older, our bank would encourage us to do the same: SAVE. They told us to keep putting all of our money into that savings account.

Deposit Account Reality

But what is happening with our money as it sits in that account? The answer is not what you may think.

Today, as your money sits in your savings account, it is actually being eroded. Whether savings account interest rates are high or low, the interest rate you get paid is never higher than the rate of inflation. Though your money is growing in numbers, your spending power is actually decreasing while you're saving. Inflation eats and consumes all the interest that you earn. That's the reality of what's happening.

When most people hear this for the first time it comes as quite a surprise to them, but once they think it through, they know it to be true. I mention it here at the beginning because I want you to know that the model of saving through the bank savings account is not beneficial to you.

First Steps In Investing

When money in a traditional savings account grows to a much larger size, your bank will usually call you or write to you and say something like "Dear Mr. Jones, we see that you now have 'x amount' of money in your bank account. Have you ever thought of investing that and making your money work harder for you?" Of course, it sounds good and sensible, so most people will agree to speak to an investment advisor.

There are two kinds of advisors. First, the ones who work for the financial institutions, and second, the independent advisors. The independent advisors will look at all investments available in the marketplace, whereas the one who works with financial institutions will only recommend their own products. In other words, investments within their own company.

When looking for a potential investor, most banks are looking for people to be solvent in the tens of thousands of dollars but there are also products that people invest in on behalf of their children that might be one or two thousand dollars. Someone else at the other end of the scale might be investing hundreds of thousands of dollars. The system is designed for all income brackets across the board. In my observation, people who are younger than thirty and have $100,000 to invest are generally happier to invest in the more risky things because it has a longer time to recover. Those who are nearing retirement place their money in less risky things, so that the money is actually there when they retire. Good examples of this would be government bonds or savings deposit accounts. But as I mentioned, those are rapidly being eroded because the rate of inflation is always higher than the interest the bank or the amount that the government pays.

Meet Your Financial Advisor

Your invitation to make your money work harder will result in a meeting where you will sit down with the advisor and they will ask you a series of questions referred to as a "fact find." Based upon how you respond to their questions, they will gauge your attitude toward risk and determine the amount of money you are willing to invest and if that amount is suitable for you. They do this in such a way that you will feel comfortable making the investment. That is the general purpose of this session. Based upon all of your responses, they will go off and research the investment market on your behalf. This research process is governed by the laws of your residence, and then they will come back to you and present you with an investment recommendation.

That type of investment is called a "buy and hold" investment. You take a specific amount of money, hand it over to them and they invest it in whatever fund it is they are recommending. All you do, as part of the process, is sign a form that allows them the power of holding and investing your money on your behalf. Though the form looks very detailed and it has a lot of small print, it basically says that you are going to pay the investment advisor a fee. If you read each line carefully, you will also see that you will be paying an annual fee to the fund manager who will be looking after your investment money. That fee is usually a percentage of the amount you invested and he will be paid whether your money goes up or down. In other words, they will always get paid, whether or not they are actually making you any money.

At that point, you have turned your money over into the hands of someone else. All you can do is sit and wait for the maturity date of that investment. The rest is out of your hands, and again, whether you are making money or not, the investment advisor and fund manager are getting paid, regardless. Pretty convenient for them, isn't it?

What Does "Buy and Hold" Actually Mean?

These types of investments are "buy and hold" investments but I have redefined them as "hope and pray" investments. I call them "hope and pray" investments because you're hoping and praying that in a number of years' time, the money that you have invested will have increased substantially and there is actually going to be a greatly increased fund of money there when you need it.

Let's say you've agreed to invest for ten years. You are going to wait for ten years and hope (and pray) that amount of invested money has gone up. Your hopes are based on past performance, even though you clearly know that past performance doesn't necessarily lead to future performance.

So in essence, you are wishing and praying things go a certain way. But you do not have a magical crystal ball. You do not know whether in ten years' time you're going to have more money or not. In fact, you cannot count on any money being there at all in the end. The only thing you can count on is that a portion of it will erode each year to pay the people taking care of it for us. That part of the arrangement is guaranteed.

If you think about this logically, it really is a *crazy system*.

You give control of your money to someone else and then hope and pray that your investment makes more money. In addition, you're going to pay someone to manage that process for you, whether they actually make money for you or not.

Is this really the best system that anyone could come up with? Is this the best financial planning vehicle for your children's college planning or your retirement planning?

Yet, that is our current investing system, yours and mine, and that is a big problem.

I will not go into more detail than that because then it would fall into the role of financial advice, and I want to make it very clear that I am *not* a financial advisor. I am sharing my opinions from my personal experience because I believe my experience and observations to be common with the experience of others. I would encourage you to always verify everything that I have experienced for yourself.

Are Financial Advisors the Problem?

No, absolutely not. I do not mean to imply that I am against financial advisors, investment advisors or fund managers. The fault I find is within the system, not the people who work within it. If you work within a system that has a rulebook, all you can do is follow the rules! In my opinion, the system is what is wrong. If you are in any of the positions above, I am sure you are doing your very best to give the best advice. But again, when the system is faulty, there is only so much you can do.

Where Has 'Buy and Hold' Mentality Left us?

This 'Buy and Hold' Mentality that we have all been brought up to believe in makes us think in a very limited way about investments and investing. Our definition of investing is we can only make money if the value of the asset that we're investing in goes up.

With the 'Buy and Hold' model, you never know whether your money is going to be there when you need it. This is basically the standard investment model in most of the western world.

What has happened to those who have put their faith in this system? It is true that some people have benefitted from good returns from this system but there are, of course, those who have not. When people have invested their hard-earned cash in this system and the value of the asset they are investing in hasn't gone up, what has happened to them? People have retired without enough money to support them. College funds have fallen short. In summary, ordinary people have encountered life-changing hardship.

The diagram on the next page clearly shows the reality of 'Buy and Hold.' If the market goes up, you make money. But in either of the other two possible directions, you lose.

These are not very good odds in anyone's book.

Buy and Hold
Reality

Stock Profit

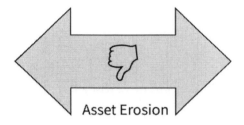

Asset Erosion

Stock Loss

What Is The Replacement for This Faulty System?

First, let's not dwell on the past. Instead, let's march brightly onto the future. The future involves benefitting from the great positive changes that have happened in the world that allow you to control your own money and your own future.

Technology has been changing and more people are beginning to take back the control of their own money management. With simple training, an electronic device and an Internet connection, you can connect anywhere, at any time and open a brokerage account with no money whatsoever. You can choose what you personally invest in yourself and manage your own investments.

Obviously, there are things to be learned, but there are plenty of people who are now doing that successfully. Not only are they managing their own finances, they are actually creating an additional income stream.

Technology has brought about a whole new world in the realm of personal money management.

The Solution

I've spent some time in this chapter outlining the dangers of both our current investing system and the fact that it has immersed us in the 'buy and hold' belief. This belief is what has held most of us back from even looking for a better alternative. Now that I have exposed the problems and faults of the current system, it's only right and proper that I propose and deliver a solution, right?

My solution lies in taking back and controlling all of your investing yourself.

But before you want to stop me with a thousand excuses of why you are not qualified for the task, let me ask you something.

> Would you like to be in control of your own financial future rather than trusting the system that we've talked about above?

If you would, then make the decision right now to investigate and read everything with an open mind, taking in all I have to share in the rest of this book.

Let me tell you more about this quiet revolution that's been taking place in investing all over the world.

The New Investment Opportunity

The advent of the Internet began to change the way we invest our money, primarily because we could do so much of our own research and also access systems we could not access before. There are hundreds of websites that give access to stock market information. Public information on all companies is readily available. We can now open a brokerage account online and control everything that happens with our investments ourselves without talking to anyone else. We can buy and sell directly in the financial markets with a simple click of a button.

The online brokerage company does take a fee each time we perform a transaction (buy or sell), but that fee is miniscule in comparison to what we would pay in traditional fees to an independent financial advisor and investment funds manager.

I have been trading online for over ten years now. I can go online and see what is happening myself.

For you then, there is no longer a need to call anyone and ask for advice. The days of calling a broker and asking what you should buy and what you should sell have become outdated. This has happened because now, you can monitor what is happening online yourself and you can take those actions yourself as well. In addition, even if you talk to a broker, all he can do is advise you the same as a financial advisor. In the end the decision is always yours.

So why is this different from how things used to be when you were first being told all about 'buy and hold' and trusting financial advisors? Obviously there is much more information accessible to you now because of the Internet. You could argue that fifteen to twenty years ago you couldn't do research on the stocks that you wanted to buy or understand how the financial markets work, but today you have access to learning resources on the Internet that are available to most people in most countries.

With this type of access, anyone can learn how to trade and more importantly, trade successfully. All you need to do is lift your head up, look around and see what advice is available. Once you do some research and gather the best advice, you can begin to take back the control of your own financial future.

This book was written to empower you to be able to make that choice.

But Isn't Trading Complicated? Can I Do It?

Most people have a specific vision of trading which they gained from television and movies. It is the image of the man sitting in front of two, three and as many as six screens watching the markets non-stop for hours, days and weeks on end. Glued to the screens with his eyes fixed and his ear to the phone. He's taking hurried calls and shouting across the trading floor. He's living on adrenaline and never gets to see his family, if he even has one.

In terms of how you can learn to trade and invest, this imagery is irrelevant rubbish and a myth. People have been led to believe that you need a lot of technology and time to trade and this is simply not true. I teach a simple program where you can learn to trade in just five minutes per day and have very positive and consistent results.

So for now, I just want you to know that you can begin with a web browser and one screen. In fact, I tell my students that if you needed to, you could trade from an Internet café or the computer at your local library. You can trade on a tablet and you can now even trade on a smartphone. (A phone isn't the ideal format, but you can do it, if needed.)

This means that as long as you have an Internet connection and a basic PC, tablet or smartphone, you will be able to trade and control your investments from anywhere in the world. How good is that?

My Story

Twelve years ago I had a regular job just like most people. I worked my way up to be a manager and the more responsibility I took on, the more hours I found myself working. I had a comfortable lifestyle with a great, privileged standard of living, but I was working far too many hours. My eldest child had just been born and I decided I didn't want to be the father that was never there. I needed to do something else with my life. It was at this point that I decided I was going to leave work and run a business myself.

That wasn't an easy choice to make, but it was a very important decision.

I wasn't a resounding success at my chosen business.
Two years later, I walked away from that first business having learned many important things but having made very little money, but not before I had started my personal development journey.

I hired a business coach during those two years who loaned me a book by Brad Sugars called *Instant Cashflow*. It was a book that I read from cover to cover in a night and it fully turned me on to what I had been missing since the day I left school—the gift of learning from others.

Brad Sugars had a list in the back of his book of suggested reading material. Enter the wonderful Mr. Tony Robbins.

After reading Tony's books and learning from his home study courses, I attended a Live Program called UPW (*Unleash the Power Within*). This was another turning point after which I decided to focus on getting my wealth building right, for the future of myself and my family.

I attended Tony Robbins' *Wealth Mastery* and that is where I first learned about trading. I listened to the advice at the seminar and I decided to attend a trading training course.

I knew from what I had learned at the seminar that being in business for myself, and trading, were the two ways I wanted to focus on to control my own financial destiny. Both seemed like a good way of earning money that was more flexible than working for somebody else. But it wasn't just about time flexibility. It was also about something much more fundamental. It was time to take control. If there is one thing that *Wealth Mastery* impressed upon me, it was this: "No one cares about your money and your financial future more than you, so you should be the one to control it."

A very powerful sentence and I encourage you to heed this message. Take control. Don't let other people who care less about your future than you be the ones who are in control of it.

Getting Through The Quicksand

Over the next few years, I developed a part-time property investing business and my trading experience went through various different formats.

This is where I started to struggle. Although I knew exactly the result that I wanted, I was in the infancy of my trading learning. I was 'wet behind the ears' as they say. There was a lot of conflicting information available and it was confusing. "This strategy works better than that strategy," and so on. I wanted to succeed but I did not know who was actually offering the best strategy and which approach would work best for me.

Because of this, I was moving from strategy to strategy and experimenting with all sorts of things. Some things worked and others didn't.

I was trying to find the best strategy that would make me as much money as possible and as fast as possible. That was what I felt I had to do because many of the books I read and the courses I attended suggested that mindset. "Make the most amount of money as fast as possible and become financially free!"

Of course it sounded great; who wouldn't want that? The people teaching the courses said, "Come and earn this kind of money, you too can be a millionaire in a few short years."

I wanted to succeed but I did not know who was actually offering the best strategy and approach. How could I be sure which one would work for me? I really had no strategy except moving from course to course, program to program, and experimenting with all sorts of things. Again, some things worked and others didn't.

As time progressed, I began to see limited success and I did make some money. Over the years, I made money from FOREX (Foreign Exchange Trading) Stocks, and Options.

Fantastic! I was really pleased with myself. However there was a 'but' and here it is: "Fantastic, I am finally making money trading, *but it is not consistent.*"

It was driving me crazy. For a number of months I would feel like I had cracked the trading code but then I would lose my focus and go on to other things in my life and then suddenly three months would have gone by and I hadn't done any trading at all.

I began to wonder what was going on. How could I turn this into a steady income flow? Why were my results so inconsistent?

My Ah-ha Moment

It took ages for the shoe to drop and what made the shoe drop was when I began to study other wealthy people through biographies and autobiographies. I was reading all of these books about wealthy people and trying to model how to be wealthy because that is what Tony Robbins had told me to do. "If you want something, find someone who already has it and model how they achieved it."

The advice made sense and that was what I had determined to do.

My 'eureka moment' came when reading a book by Felix Dennis called *How to Get Rich*.

Felix Dennis has a publishing empire in the United Kingdom. I have absolutely no idea how well he's known as he is outside of my own country, but *How to Get Rich* is a very entertaining and frank book full of business wisdom tips interspersed with the interesting story of his life.

The most important message for me was towards the end of the book. In brief, what he was saying was that he was having a great life. He was 'retired' and he now wrote poetry and he did poetry talks and tours. He said that that is what he loved to do.

In addition to doing the thing that made him most happy, writing poetry, he said that he could have anything he wanted in terms of what money could buy. To illustrate this he described that he was writing his book in his cottage, which was in the Caribbean Island of St. Lucia, and he could look out over the ocean each time he was writing. As he was doing this – looking out over the ocean as he was putting the finishing touches to this book – he posed this question: "Although I've got everything I want in terms of what money can buy, would I give it all away now, to be young again?"

And he said, "Absolutely I would, in a flash."

That was *the* moment.

A sudden realization hit me and has never left me since.

The most important asset in the world is *time*. It can never be replaced.

I had a good, long look at myself and at what the world had taught me to do. Culture and society teach us to spend huge amounts of life's most precious asset – time – trying to build up a great amount of money.

And what would we all gladly do when we are in our senior years and we've made all this money?

Yes, my friends, we would gladly give it all away just to be young again and have the time back. Precious time that we spent (or wasted) chasing and making the money in the first place.

I immediately recognized the Catch-22.

Where was the way out of this conundrum?

Let me share what I came up with.

If time is the most important of life's gifts, then where does money come in? Well, it depends upon what you want to do with your time.

I realized that I shouldn't be chasing the big money. What I should be doing is finding out how to make a consistent amount of money expending the smallest amount of time possible. That was actually the objective.

The powerful shift was when I went from "make the most amount of money as fast as possible" to "spend the least amount of time and make a consistent amount of money".

I wanted to be freed up from working, whether that meant for someone else or in my own business. I realized I wanted to spend time with my family and the last thing I wanted with my own business was to mimic the scenario I had when I had an employer.

Finding the Solution

I made a decision to go back to everything I had learned about trading and to find or create my own ultimate trading solution.

The greatest secret to trading successfully and consistently is to find a strategy that fits in with you and your lifestyle.

Below are the key questions I asked myself.
What strategy can I do that...

- only takes five minutes a day?
- will earn me money consistently?
- is really low risk?
- doesn't need a lot of management?

You see, the answer to this series of questions has given me the perfect balance to my life.

I also believe it will give anyone a fantastic life because it gives you the precious commodity of time and a consistent income.

I have to confess that the solution didn't just come from my trading knowledge. It came from my property knowledge as well. Allow me to explain in the next section.

What You Can Learn from Property Investors

There are a huge amount of people who buy property as a capital investment – they 'buy and hold'.

Remember when I shared the 'Buy and Hold' diagram? It is important so I am sharing it again on the following page. You can clearly see that if the market goes up, you make money. But in either of the other two possible directions, you lose.

Again, these are not very good odds in anyone's book.

Buy and Hold
Reality

Stock Profit

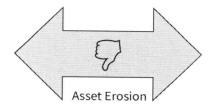

Asset Erosion

Stock Loss

However, there are a large percentage of property investors who adopt a very different approach.

These investors ensure that they only buy property where the property has a good chance of going up in value, such as in a location of high demand. They also make sure that the income coming in from rental income far exceeds the costs that are payable on the property.

In other words, they make a monthly net profit on their property just from rent alone.

The following diagram is what their property investment looks like to them.

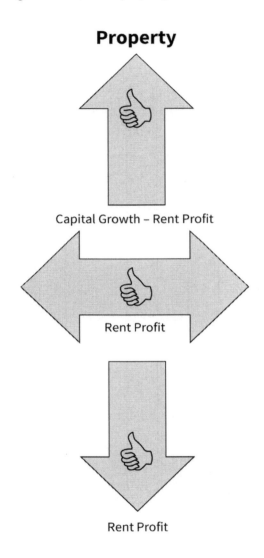

Property

Capital Growth – Rent Profit

Rent Profit

Rent Profit

If the property goes up in value, the property investor gains an increase in capital value and, in addition, they also gain a net profit from their rental income after costs.

If the property market is just going sideways in the area they have their property, that is, it's not going up but it's not falling, they still get a monthly profit from the rental income after costs.

If the property market in that area is taking a temporary dip in value and it's going down, they still get a monthly profit from the rental income after costs.

So what have they achieved with this strategy?

They are making a monthly income whether the property market goes up, whether the property market stays the same, and they even make money when the property market goes down.

Isn't that a brilliant strategy?

Hats off to this group of property investors!

This property approach is what we're going to apply to the world of stock trading.

Your opportunity in the stock market is to make a monthly income on your stocks whether the stock goes up, down, or stays the same, just like the property investors do.

The diagram on the following page shows what we can achieve with *The Cashflow Trader* method.

Cashflow Trader Method

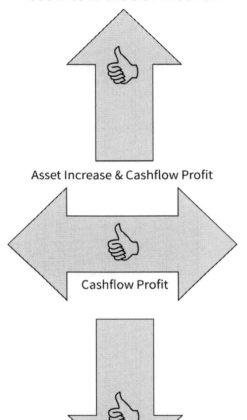

Asset Increase & Cashflow Profit

Cashflow Profit

Cashflow Profit

This is a vast improvement on the 'buy and hold' model.

Everyone else is still hanging onto the 'buy and hold' model even though there are much better ways of trading. They do so purely because that is all they know.

Now you know different, that there is a better way.

But before we get into the detail of how to make this consistent cash flow, I have much more to tell you about the obstacles that traders face and how to avoid them.

Chapter Two – The Danger of Emotions (Fear & Greed)

The second obstacle to successful trading is emotions. In order to understand emotions in trading, I will start by discussing the concept of 'the herd'. To begin, I will start with an example from nature.

The Herd

This is a history lesson about the hunting of buffalo by the Native Americans. When the native people arrived in America after crossing the Bering Strait from Siberia, the buffalo were a huge problem to them. They were nomadic animals that wandered across the vast plains of America and they were migratory, so they got in the way quite often.

The buffalo were originally hunted using bows, arrows, lances or spears. The buffaloes were a very fierce animal and were difficult to tackle. Hunting them with such primitive weapons was ineffective and very dangerous.

Then the Native Americans discovered something very interesting about buffalo. They observed how individual buffalo behaved in a herd when the herd was panicked. When a buffalo is panicked, it puts its head down and charges forward, only paying attention to what it can see in its peripheral vision at the left and right side of its head in response to what all the other buffalo are doing around it. At no point in this process does it actually look up and see what's ahead of it. This was the key that the Native Americans had been looking for.

Armed with this information, they adopted a new hunting method. They would surround the buffalo on horseback and slowly move the herd toward a cliff or a precipice. They would then panic the herd and the herd would stampede. The stampeding herd, not looking where it was going, would go straight over the precipice and there was a huge kill of multiple buffaloes. This would happen without any of the dangers of hunting individual buffalo.

That is a great lesson about herd behavior in the animal world. So, let me ask you a question, and this question is the key in trading.

Do humans do the same?

Do they behave in a herd-like manner in certain situations?

The answer is.......... Yes.
When we look at stock prices, the point here is that the share price is often a result of emotional and herd-like behavior in the market. It is very seldom based on pure logic.

Let me give you an example of this.

The Northern Rock Crisis

We had an event in the United Kingdom that was referred to as "The Northern Rock Crisis."

Northern Rock was a British bank, most recently owned and operated by Virgin Money. It was based at Regent Centre in Newcastle upon Tyne, United Kingdom. During 2012, the Northern Rock brand was phased out and replaced by Virgin. Northern Rock was best known for becoming the first bank in 150 years to suffer a bank run after having had to approach the Bank of England for a loan facility, to replace money market funding, during the credit crisis in 2007. Having failed to find a commercial buyer for the business, it was taken into public ownership in 2008, and was then bought by Virgin Money in 2012.

What is a Bank Run?

A bank run (better known as 'a run on the bank') takes place in a fractional reserve banking system when a huge number of bank customers or depositors line up outside a bank to collect their deposits from the financial institution simultaneously, either in cash demand or transfer of funds into investment portfolios like government bonds, precious stones or metals, or even to a reliable financial institution. They do this because they are convinced that the bank is, or might become, insolvent.

As more and more individuals withdraw their money or deposits, the chances of a fail to pay increases, consequently sets off even more withdrawals. This can wreck the bank to the level where it runs out of funds and, therefore, faces unexpected bankruptcy or insolvency.

This threat of the bank running out of money as more and more depositors panic can take the bank under.

I watched the television as the Bank of England faced a parliamentary committee about this crisis. They were answering the question of whether the Bank of England could have done anything more. The Bank of England politely pointed out to the group of members of Parliament, who were questioning them about what happened, that in this scenario it was Parliament who had passed the law which stated that if a bank got in trouble (in this case the Northern Rock), they had an obligation to let everybody know.

In other words, they must make the information public.

Obviously, the information that the bank was in trouble going public caused everyone to line up outside every branch of the bank to get their money out and this put the bank in more trouble. Eventually the bank went totally under.

The important point about this particular incident that is relevant to this situation is that as investors in the bank panicked, investors in Northern Rock shares in the stock market did the same. People sold their shares like crazy and the price of the Northern Rock stock fell dramatically.

What would have happened if no one was aware the bank was in trouble? What if the press would not have been able to tell anyone about it?

The Bank of England would have given The Northern Rock the necessary resources they needed to slowly get themselves out of the mess they were in. Then by improving and making their banking practices more secure, they would have recovered overtime and no one would have been any the wiser.

In other words, all of the investors' money in the bank would have been safe.

What this example shows us is that sometimes making information public makes people behave in a herd-like manner, which often has huge effects. This applies not only in the business realm, but in all sorts of things in society; and in this particular case, on the stock price and the stock market as well.

Why Do Traders Get So Emotional?

Traders get emotional because they put themselves in situations where they are more inclined to exhibit an emotional response.

Let me give you an example. Many private traders like to emulate what they perceive as the trading behavior of professional traders.

This is what they do. They sit in front of the trading screen all day or for many hours a day trying to predict what will happen on a certain stock or asset class. Once they select a trading opportunity and enter into it, they get to watch the trade progress on the screen in front of them. The price of the asset class they've chosen to trade in moves. Sometimes the trade moves many times a day, sometimes many times a minute, between profitability and loss. The trade moves into the money, then out of the money, then into the money again, then out of the money again, and time and time again, this can repeat.

Now if you had a wallet full of cash resting on the outcome of the trade and you were constantly swinging between making money and losing money, I'm sure you would begin to get pretty stressed out and that is exactly what is happening to these people, day after day after day.

When the mind is experiencing that loss-or-win type of stress, even hardened traders find it difficult to do the right thing.

Let me ask another question.

Why do so many people invest when the market is high?

The answer is that when the market was low, they were fearful that it would go lower so they didn't buy, but when the market goes higher, their greed or desire for more kicks in and they invest. They think that the market is going to go to the moon and never come back.

After they have invested at the high point, they find the market soon turns around and moves lower and they find themselves facing a loss.

Below is a fictitious example to illustrate how emotions can wreak havoc on your trading.

Let's say we have a company and we will call it Corporation 2020.

Let's say Corporation 2020 has had its annual accounts performed and it has a very clear book value of $1 billion, which has been audited and verified.

Then let's say that Corporation 2020 launches for the first time on the stock market and its initial public offering (IPO) is 1 billion shares.

So everybody agrees the company is worth 1 billion dollars. And, as we are issuing 1 billion shares, the value of each of those shares is logically one dollar.

The reality of the situation on the stock market is that as soon as that share is launched, there will immediately be an opinion that is emotionally driven by various people in the markets who want to buy that share that will make its price move on the stock market away from one dollar.

It is commonplace in the stock market for share values to go from a position of underbought (that is they are below a price that is commonly believed to be the true value of the share), and move to a price that is overbought (which is above the commonly believed true value of the share).

As we move from the lower price in the underbought position, to the higher price of the overbought position, the herd mentality kicks in at various points.

I will explain this cycle using the following diagrams.

Price Action vs. Logic

$

20

         Over Priced

17.50

15.00 -

12.50

10.00 ●

         Under Valued

The focus point is the middle dotted line.

It's not clearly defined, but let's say this is a price that most people agree is the rough value of the stock.

Price Action vs. Logic

$

20
          Over Priced

17.50

15.00 -

12.50

10.00
          Under Valued

At $10 the stock is cheap, undervalued; so sophisticated investors buy because they know it will go up eventually.

Generally a lot of unsophisticated investors sit on the sidelines at this point in the cycle because the stock is low in value and they see it has the potential to go lower. (Unsophisticated investors are more prone to fear.)

However, the sophisticated investors see that it has the potential to go higher. They begin to buy into the stock. They are buying in large volumes.

As they start buying, the stock becomes more in demand and the price rises. This is simple economics - the law of supply and demand.

Price Action vs. Logic

$

20

Over Priced

17.50

15.00 -

12.50

10.00

Under Valued

The price now rises to a point where even the most casual and unsophisticated observer can see that the stock is recovering in price and it's doing well.

At this point the less sophisticated investors, 'the herd', start following the initial investors and they start buying when the price is high. The people who buy at the bottom are the market makers. The people who buy past the middle line are the herd.

This activity takes the share price to a point where it's overbought ($17.50). The price of a share of this stock is higher than it naturally should be.

How do sophisticated investors view this position?

Price Action vs. Logic

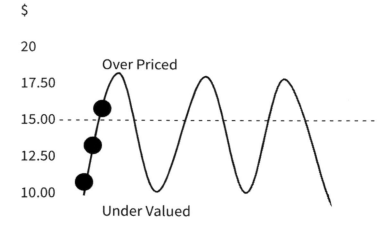

This is the point where they consider they've made some good money on the stock. At this point they start selling. They sell in large numbers; this makes the stock more readily available, but there is initially still plenty of demand for what they sell as the herd is still buying.

The price goes up temporarily to peak ($18.50 in the diagram) but quickly the rally runs out of steam and the selling continues. There is more supply than demand and therefore the price starts dropping from its high.

As the price falls, the unsophisticated investor holds onto his stock, as he is fearful of losing money. He bought high and is hoping this is a small drop in price that won't last.

As the price falls below the logical common value, the unsophisticated traders panic and start selling their stock at a loss. The herd mentality kicks in again.

They think, "Everyone else is selling the stock so I must too."

Despite their best intentions of buying low and selling high, what in fact happens to most unsophisticated investors and traders is that they buy high and sell low.

What we have just described is a perfect example of how emotion deceives a huge proportion of traders at every turn.

It is the sophisticated investors who apply logic and systems who win out every time.

There are few things more guaranteed to engage the emotion of the human being than money. We argue with our spouses about it, we argue with our friends about it, we can even sometimes be found arguing with ourselves about it. We seem to be in a dispute about how best it can be spent, how it should be used, or how we can avoid losing it. Most people will do more to avoid losing money than they will to make some.

So now that we've seen what can go wrong when our emotion kicks in let's get to the solution.

Solution

How do you keep your emotions at bay?

- You use a strategy that doesn't keep you in front of your trading screen all day. Less time in front of your trading screen means less emotion and, therefore, less stress, less hassle and ultimately, less losing trades.

- You select a strategy that has a very quick and clear approach to making a trading decision. If your strategy has a clear signal, it is much quicker to take action on your trading decision and, therefore, spend a lot less time watching the market with your emotions engaged.

- You use a strategy where you only need to trade once a month.

- You make sure the effort required is minimal and the risk is low. If you chase big returns in the market, then ultimately you take on too much risk. If you take on too much risk, you start having sleepless nights, or at the very least, you engage 'stress mode' as you trade. If you have minimal effort and adopt a low risk approach, trading is a calm and stress-free experience, and consistent results follow naturally.

Because trading is primarily concerned with making money or avoiding the loss of money, understanding how emotions can affect our trading performance is a key skill that when mastered, will lead to great success.

People fail at the stock market because they attach too much emotion to it. They tightly clench their fists, furrow their brows and say, "I've got to beat the market.

It's out there waging a war against me. I'm trying to make money and it's trying to stop me."

It is as if it's "man against market and market against man."

This is how many people see it. Some have fear, others need control, and others still are fueled by greed. I can tell you now, these emotions will not make you a successful trader. They will not serve you. Emotionally, you must disconnect from seeing the market as an entity that is out to get you or something that must submit to your will. The people who have this view of the stock market fail.

The market is not, and cannot, be driven by your emotions, so you are better off if you can disconnect your emotions from trading. I know it may be difficult at first, because after all, that is your money on the line, but try to stay calm and take the opportunities that the market provides you with.

When you learn to stay calm, you have a strategy and a process that you go through every day, and you will eventually learn to see the best opportunities. If the opportunities are there: take them. If they are not, then don't trade.

It really is that simple.

Stay calm.

The people who are very good at trading are ones who stay calm and take the opportunities the market provides.

Chapter Three – Leverage

The third obstacle to successful trading is leverage. Let me show you why people use leverage first, and then I will share why it is a danger to traders and investors.

You can use leverage as a tool when you invest. I will use the example of buying a house, as it is something most people can relate to. There are two common ways to purchase this house: an outright purchase of the whole property with cash, or with using a cash deposit and a mortgage. Most of us choose the latter. We put a small amount of money down and the rest comes from the bank in the form of a mortgage. This is because most of us cannot afford to purchase the house outright.

Before we look at the leveraged example of a house purchase, let's look at an example of a house purchase that is not leveraged.

House Purchase Without Leverage

If we buy a house in cash for $100,000 and wait for it to double in price to $200,000, then what is our percentage return on our initial investment of $100,000?

To work out our percentage ROI, you divide your return by your initial investment and multiply the result by one hundred. The easy way to remember this is:

> Money In divided by Money Out = A, then multiply A by 100 to get your percentage of profit or loss.

In this case, our money in is the increase in value of the property, which is $100,000 divided by the money out, the $100,000 you initially invested.

The total of this sum is 1.
Then you multiple this by 100.

This gives us 100%.

I'm sure you could have worked that out in your head, but it helps to show how to work out your percentage return on investment.

House Purchase Using Leverage

Now let's look at an example of leverage.

Let's say you buy the same house for a purchase price of $100,000.

You pay a down payment of $25,000 and you borrow the other $75,000 from the bank.

Now, let's do the same as before and wait for the house to double in value.

We make a $100,000 purchase again, the same amount, but this time you have only invested $25,000 of your own money.

To work out your percentage ROI in this case, you divide your return by your initial investment and multiple by 100. Remember this is money in divided by the money out and multiply the total by 100.

So in this leveraged example, the increase in value of the property is $100,000.

Divided by the $25,000 you initially invested, the total of this sum is 4.

You then multiple this number by 100.

This gives us 400%!

Using this property example, you can clearly see why investors all over the world love leverage!

Most people agree that property holds its value very well and if it drops it is renowned for recovering over time. For this reason, leverage never becomes a disadvantage in property investing.

Leverage in Trading Is Much Different

However, leverage in trading works differently because you can lose money as fast as you make it. This is because the market moves in three directions: up, down and sideways.

If the market moves against you, the leverage effect works against you, too.

Trading Without Leverage

Let me give you an example:

Let's say you buy a share for $100 and after research you are expecting it to move to $120.

Again, look at the non-leveraged example first to see if it does what you expect and it rises in price to $120.

What would be your percentage return on investment?

Money in, which is $20, divided by money invested, which is $100.

This gives you a total of 0.20, which you multiply by 100 to give you 20%.

Now let's look at the potential downside:

In theory, what can happen to the price of your stock?

Well, of course it can go down in value. Let's say if the stock went down by $20 you would sell it because you wanted to limit your potential loss to $20.

If it went down to this point and you sold for $80, your loss would be $20.

You can work out your percentage loss in the same way as you worked out your percentage profit.

Your return is now a negative number, minus $20, and you divide this by your money invested, which was $100.

This gives you a total of minus 0.20, which you then multiply by 100 to give you a loss of -20%.

Trading Using Leverage

Now let's look at both examples from a leveraged position:

Apply a leverage of four times to your example. Remember, you buy a share for $100 and it rises in price to $120. But because you apply leverage of 4 times, then you only need $25 for a $100 investment. When the stock goes up by $20 you make a $20 profit leveraged 4 times.

In this case, what would be your percentage return on investment?

Money in, which is $20 divided by money invested, which is $25.

This gives you a total of 0.80, which you multiply by 100 to give you 80%.

Now, look at your potential downside when leveraged by four times:

You limit your potential loss to $20.

If the stock price fell to $80 and you sold for $80, what would be your loss?

Let's calculate your leveraged loss.

You can work out your percentage loss in the same way as you worked out your percentage profit.

Your return is now a negative number, minus $20, and you divide this by your money in, which was $25. This gives you a total of minus 0.80, which you multiply by 100 to give you a loss of 80%!

So leverage is not so great while investing in stock when it works against you. Though, not many of the 'get rich quick' guys will point that out to you.

This may leave you wondering where leverage comes from in stock investing.

The answer is, from specialist products in the market that brokers provide to allow you to use leverage.

Considering there are products on the market that allow you to use 100 times leverage, imagine how quickly you could zero your account if you get things wrong!

It goes without saying that if you can use leverage to gain quick profits, it can also come back and take them from you. Even with a good strategy, losses can be substantial.

If you've got the right strategy, then leverage is great, but if the strategy is too complex and difficult to execute perfectly every time, then it can wipe out your account, and this is what happens to countless people.

To summarize, leveraging can be great when it builds your account quickly. But it is clearly a danger if it can also harm you and wipe out your account.

High leverage always means high risk, and there's no getting away from that.

Solution

So what is my solution to this leverage problem?

Use a strategy that doesn't rely on leverage to give good returns.

There are strategies in the market that give consistent returns without the need for leverage. Again, if you don't chase massive returns and you are happy with regular, smaller but consistent returns, you can still build up true wealth.

If you must use leveraged products, then use them in a way that can't take money out of your account.

Chapter Four – Overly Complex Strategies

The Fourth obstacle to successful trading is overly complex trading strategies.

Something you will want to avoid from the start is anything that is overly complex. An overly complex strategy is just as it sounds, overly complex. They usually require too much time, and too much thought to execute. If it is not simple and easy to do, you will not be able to do it on a regular basis.

In order to explain what I mean by 'overly complex strategy' I am going to demonstrate what I consider to be overly complex.

Those of you who have not traded before may not recognize some of the following terminology but do not worry about that now, because if you trade my way you will never need to understand it anyway. I do not mean to be flippant, but it is true.

Those of you who have traded before will recognize some of these terms and you will be able to relate to some of the trouble that they cause.

Too Many Indicators

The first ingredient of an overly complex strategy is the use of too many indicators.

For those who have not heard this term before, an indicator is something that can be employed in trading software that gives you a visual numerical view of some aspect of the historical price movement of a stock.

What an indicator tries to do is predict the future by looking at the price patterns and volume patterns of the past.

As you know, past performance is not an indicator of future performance on any given stock in the stock market, or any commodity anywhere.

An indicator can only use past data. Remember, no one has a magic crystal ball. Yet despite this, many people rely on numerous indicators in their trading strategy. I do not mean to say that the indicators do not help or do not have their uses, but one of the problems is that people who invent trading strategies sometimes use four or five different indicators to give them a trading decision or to point to a trading opportunity. In my opinion, for someone who is new to trading, this is a huge amount to learn, and in a lot of cases, it is completely unnecessary.

I am not being glib or irreverent. Remember, I have tried a number of different trading solutions and styles over my ten-plus years in trading. Through experience, I can tell you that trading strategies using many indicators are not going to help you get your trading done in five minutes a day. They are not going to let you earn money in the first month, either. This is because it takes a lot of time to learn how to use four or five indicators well enough to base a trade on.

Too Much Investigation

The next ingredient in an overly complex trading strategy is too much investigation before you trade.

Some trading strategies require you to spend hours of research on the stock or the type of trade you're going to make before you have enough information to know whether to enter the trade or not.

This investigation requires an investment of too much time before you place your trade, as well as requiring you to keep looking at the screen, waiting for a good period of time because you know there's an opportunity coming, but the opportunities are not there yet.

If you have never tried sitting down and looking at a trading screen for two hours, waiting for something to happen, then you cannot truly appreciate the phrase "it's like watching paint dry." Because that is exactly what it's like.

I like to have fun in my life and that is certainly not fun. I am sure that you have much better things to do with your valuable and precious time than to sit and stare at a screen all day.

Too Stressful

At the other end of the scale, some trading strategies can be complex because they have to be done in a very short amount of time. For example, there is a strategy in Forex trading, that is currency trading for those of you haven't done it before, which is called 'scalping'.

The idea in scalping is to make money from very quick or short moves in the market. For instance, getting in and out of a trade in five seconds.

For those of you who have not tried trading before, does that sound like a nice, stress-free, calm thing to do?

Of course not. Scalping is anything but stress free.

There are also plenty of trading strategies that claim you can make six to ten percent per month.

That sounds fantastic, doesn't it?

That is the sort of trading strategy I went after when I first started. What you don't know at the time of getting into these is that in order to make such amounts of money per month, you have to do many trades per month. Each of those trades also carries a high risk – you can make that money or you can lose it. And again, the more trades you make each month requires more time that you need to put into those trades.

I am sure that by now you know my beliefs on the balance of time and money. If you didn't grasp it yet, the goal is to go for something that takes less time and makes consistent money. Doing many trades does not happen without a large investment of time.

There is also another factor that most novices do not plan for.

When you have multiple trades each month, the trades overlap. So while you are looking for new trading opportunities to make money from, you are also managing the trade you started on a few days ago. Therefore, you are trying to manage a number of different things at once.

Here is where you need to ask yourself an important question.

Are you any good at juggling?

Because if you aren't, this could be a real problem, real quick.

The Solution - Keep It Simple

The solution to this problem is really straightforward. You need to find a simple strategy. Asking a good question is the best place to begin.

What Does A Simple Strategy Look Like?

- Let's say you only needed to use one indicator. That there is just one signal you need in order for you to know if it is the right time to trade. That would be good, wouldn't it?

- What if you only had to make one trade each month to make the money you needed to make? Again, I'm hoping I'm getting your thumbs up here.

- There is a long time frame in which your signal is available. What I mean by this is that instead of having to look for a signal at a specific time, on a specific day, and needing to sit in front of the PC at that time, you are actually working with a strategy that has a good signal which is there for most of the trading day. This means that you could choose any time of the day to go to that trading chart and your signal would be there. If your signal is there, obviously you would trade. If your signal is not there, you close your PC and go on to do something more exciting, not needing to come back again until the next day.

- That would be a simple way to look for a trading signal, wouldn't it?

The good news is that is exactly what these simple trading strategies are about.

I use them month in, month out, and so do my students to create consistent cash flow without any of the fuss and worry that is normally associated with trading.

Chapter Five – Not Having a Big Enough Reason Why

This chapter covers the fifth obstacle to successful trading. One of the major factors that contribute to your ability to be successful in anything in life is one key thing. Can you guess what it is?

The one key thing is your reason why.

Let me ask you a question.

Why do you want to be financially free?

Take a few moments to write down your answer right now.

_____
_____
_____
_____
_____
_____

Do you know that one of the greatest obstacles to being a successful trader is not having enough of a reason why?

It sounds simple and even unrelated, yet trust me when I tell you that it is a huge factor in trading discipline.

I know a number of traders and also a number of property investors who have plenty of strategies and ways of making money, but they never seem to make any more money than they have right now, even though they have all the tools to do so.

Why do they struggle?

The reason they don't make more money even though they know how, is because they haven't got a big enough driving force. In other words, they don't have a big enough reason why in their life that drives them on to be consistent, to persevere, and to make sure everything happens day after day to lead them to a better lifestyle. They are "comfortable" where they are and they are not thinking about or conscious of planning effectively for the future.

When I ask my students to write down why they want to be financially free, various answers come back and here are some of the more common examples:

"I want to be financially free."
"I'd like a better lifestyle at retirement."
"I want money to leave to my children, for their security."
"I want to give to my favorite charity."
"I want to travel when I get older."
"I want security."
"I want freedom."

Doesn't everyone want the above things?

Yes. We all want those things, and the answers are really good. Most of us can agree with all of those reasons, and that is the problem. The answers above are all too generic.

The reason why just isn't strong enough!

I also get the students who tell me what they don't want.

"I don't want to work anymore."
"I don't want to live in this small house."
"I don't want to be stuck at home while all of my friends enjoy vacations and cruises."

Do you think it is productive to focus on what you don't want?

Of course not.

If you say to someone, "Okay, you can have your perfect lifestyle tomorrow with the wave of a magic wand. What does that perfect lifestyle look like?" Most people can't tell you in any sort of detail.

Again, a stronger reason why and more detail is essential.

The Solution – Get Specific

Let me give you an example: "I want a better retirement lifestyle."

What does that mean exactly, and more specifically, what does that mean to you?

When you jot down your answer, I want you to expand upon it. What does a better retirement lifestyle look like to you? Get as specific as you possibly can.

What are you doing when you're retired? Where are you living? Where do you like to eat? How much does it cost to pay the bills where you're living? How much does it cost to eat out at your favorite restaurant? How many times a month will you do that? How much do you need each year for health care when you retire? What kind of car do you drive? Where are you going in that car every day? How much gas do you need? What's the cost of that gas?

You must break it down into a very specific number or budget so you have a real target to move towards. "I want a nice retirement" is not enough. It is too vague and generic because we all want that. The point is, how much will be necessary for your specific retirement, exactly the way you want to experience it.

The questions are really quite basic and I hope you can see what I'm getting at. If I start asking all those questions and you actually write down how much money you need for your ideal lifestyle or your comfortable retirement, then you've actually got a real number to aim for.

That is part one of the plan; you need to know exactly how much money you need.

The great thing about going through this process and asking all these questions is that you get a very clear picture in your mind of exactly what you want. The more your goal is clearly defined, the better chance you have of attaining that goal.

How about Part Two of the plan?

What will you do once you have the money?

Another thing that occurs when you have more money is that a natural result of that is to have more time.

More time = time freedom.

How are you going to spend that extra time? What does that extra time represent to you? What will you do with that extra time? Learn to cook? Learn to paint? Take classes? Volunteer? Travel? Where are you going to do this? How long will it take each day, each week? How often will you partake in this? What is the specific budget needed for this new activity? Are you going to have to invest in tools or materials? How much do they cost?

The same way you begin to think about the finances in specific detail, you also need to think about the time in specific detail.

How will you spend your time and what are the costs necessary to do so? Think on this and write your answers below.

_____
_____
_____
_____
_____
_____

Create the focus and detail around what the money will actually give you. Having this detailed list will act as a map and it will drive you much more than a very simple focus on "I want to have more money."

Finding Your Reason

So what if you had that money now? What would you do with it?

When I do this exercise in my classes, I am surprised how people cannot answer this simple question. You see, they have been so focused on getting the money that they've never thought about what happens when they actually have it. I see students who, despite the fact that it only takes five minutes a day, will not take that time to do it and make all sorts of excuses. Yet, I am sure most people would agree that we can all find five minutes a day.

If they're not trading consistently, I've found that they don't have a big enough *reason* to do it. They don't have a big enough *why*. They're basically happy with their life as it is and therefore, they do not have a strong reason for changing and that's why they're not actually changing.

Although they say they want more money, this, that and the other, they're actually quite happy doing what they're doing.

When I explain why investing makes so much sense, I remind people of the things they said they wanted to do. If you remind yourself why you are doing it, it makes it easier to learn the process and take the time to do it. In other words, the process is simpler when you remind yourself why you are doing this to begin with.

When you are in the midst of living your life and going through your daily motions, you most likely do not consciously think about the future. You have your work, your family, your friends and it is easy to spend your time thinking of them and their needs now. What I am suggesting is that you begin thinking of their future needs as well as their immediate needs.

The Solution

You absolutely must get detailed on this and give it serious consideration. The stronger your reason why, the better you will be at trading. You will be more committed because you will be focused on your aim and your desired outcome.

You must be fully committed to your trading. You have to make sure that you understand that five minutes a day means each and every single day. I need to know, and you need to know, that you're going to commit to doing things five minutes each and every day. You absolutely have to, otherwise it is not going to work.

Knowing your why is what will push you through to honor that commitment. It is what will keep you focused when other things could potentially get in the way.

Knowing your why is what will MAKE YOU DO IT!

Do you know that most employers have a preference for who they hire?

They do.

They prefer to employ people who have spouses, children and mortgage payments. The reason should be obvious after what we've just discussed. The spouse, the children and the mortgage payment is a very good reason and WHY for them to show up at work consistently each and every day.

Does that make sense?

I hope that makes really good sense to you because truly understanding the power of your belief system and why, is a key element to trade successfully. Once you have that written down, I suggest you go even deeper. Not just to have a better life for the spouse and the children, and to have more security of a better home and so on. Get into the details. What does a better life for them specifically look like?

Write actual things down when you think about having a nice life or a good life. Describe it in as much detail as you can. Go in depth and get very personal with it. Imagine it so strongly in your mind that you have a clear picture in your mind and then write down everything you see.

I can ask you to spend 10 minutes on this task but, really, this is about the rest of your life.

For the sake of practice, I ask that you stop now and take at least 10 minutes to complete this exercise. Write down exactly why you are doing what you are doing.

Specifically write how you want your life to be, exactly, and how trading will assist in that. Trading may only be one part of it. For instance, I invest in both property and in trading, so trading forms part of my life plan, not all of my life plan. I want you to understand where trading fits within your life plan and what parts of your life it will contribute to. What are you expecting out of it and what is it going to contribute towards?

Do not only write down money and financial figures. Instead, write down the actual experiences you are going to have in your life based on what you are going to learn and accomplish by trading. All of these things will help you have a better reason why, and a better reason why means you will be more committed. Having a stronger reason why means you are going to be a more successful trader.

If you have not stopped yet to take the ten minutes to begin writing, please do so now. I cannot stress the importance of this exercise. I also encourage you to spend at least 30 minutes per week thinking about your why. Check in with yourself regularly, and remind yourself why you are doing this. Ask questions of yourself, questions like "how can I improve my plan for my life? What can I add to my list? What more detail can I add to it to make it more real to me - to make me really want it?"

Part One Conclusion

I know that I may have touched on some concepts in these first five chapters which may not be familiar to you. I have done this to help you understand that while you may have one picture in your mind about investing, there are always two sides to the story. I want you to understand that obstacles do exist. I also want you to understand that they can be overcome and that you can make a healthy and consistent income from trading.

What would a 20% return on your investments every year for the rest of your life mean to you? Just think about it. 1.5% per month compounded is all that is necessary to achieve a 20% return each year. If I can do that and *The Cashflow Trader Program* students can do it, then I know that you can do it, too!

I know when you implement what you learn in this book, that it will lead you to a more carefree life, where you are in control. Remember, this isn't just about money; it's about freedom and choice. You don't have to invest where everyone else tells you, nor do you have to trust someone else with your financial future. You can be in control, you can be profitable and you can reach your destination sooner, enjoying the journey and time freedom while you get there!

PART TWO

Part Two will cover trading as an Individual. It will introduce you to trading basics and also introduce you to the world of options trading. It will explain how most people use options in the market and why you are not going to do things that way. It will show you how to adopt a low risk approach into a very safe 'starter' option strategy, a strategy that will create a monthly income for you from the stock market.

Chapter Six - Trading as an Individual

There are many people who think the only way to trade successfully is to emulate the traders in the city.

They immediately have an image of 'big' people who trade with 'big' money, but that's really not necessary.

Let me give you an analogy.

Pretend you are Jack in the fairy tale *Jack and the Beanstalk*. Being Jack, you will remember that you swapped your cow for some magical beans. After a very good ticking off from your mother, you planted the beans in the back garden and went to sleep.

When you woke up the next morning there was a great new opportunity awaiting you. You couldn't wait to climb all the way up the massive beanstalk to find out what new opportunities were waiting for you in this strange new land up in the sky.

As you explore the giant's castle, imagine that you find the giant's dining room. You peek around the door, and you see the back of the giant sitting at a grand dining table, far across the room. You can tell from the fantastic smells that are tempting you that on the table there is a huge meal laid out. You know it is the most food you have ever dreamed of. You can hear the giant chewing and you wish you could get your hands on all that food and take it home. You are starving, and you are tempted by everything the giant's table has to offer.

If you wanted some of the food that was on the plate, you could take a huge risk and climb the legs of the giant's table and try and creep close to the plate to steal some food. But that path would be full of risk, and although the reward could be huge, the risks could be catastrophic.

In my opinion, those in trading who try to emulate the 'big' traders in the city and go after huge wins and try and make their fortune in a year are doing this. They are scrambling up the leg of the table and running across the table to grab a massive chicken leg from the huge plate and attempting to drag it off the table before the giant sees them.

The reality is that the giant *will* see them and the high risk strategy they have adopted will be their end. That giant's hand is going to come down on them sometime and stop them eating forever.

So what's the alternative?

Take the low risk strategy. Ask yourself, do you even need the massive chicken leg on the plate? What would be a safer way of getting everything you need and making sure you could keep it forever?

Here's what you could do. You could wait, hidden and safe and away from danger at the foot of the giant's chair. You could wait to pick up the crumbs that fall from the giant's table. They may only be crumbs to the giant, but to you, they are enough. When they fall down, they are big enough for you, and over time, they will amount to a huge stockpile of food. The giant will never see you down there and you can keep coming back for more, totally unobserved.

Wouldn't that be a much wiser option?

This is my secret to trading.

Do not gamble and do not take the high risk approach.

It really isn't necessary in order to achieve your aim.

Resolve to just take from the market when it presents you with an opportunity and make sure you are looking for it regularly. You need to check in just once a day, making sure you take the gifts that the market presents to you. Do not enter into high risk territory in the hopes of making a killing, which is more likely to crush you than give you good results.

Just be patient and take the crumbs that the giant leaves. These crumbs are more than enough to keep you satisfied.

So let's begin.

Chapter Seven - Trading Basics

In this section on trading basics, I'm going to show you how to read price information on a trading chart and also highlight the difference between two different types of analysis. The two types of analysis are technical analysis and fundamental analysis.

Reading A Stock Chart

When you trade you will always need information about the price of the particular stock or asset class that you are looking at. Depending on your strategy of choice, you may need to check this several times a day or just once a day. Whatever the need, it is obviously important that you understand how to read price action (or price movement) on a trading chart.

Price and Volume

Remember when I discussed emotion in Chapter Two? I shared the fact that emotion drives and has a huge influence on the price of stocks in the market. When you look at the chart, you are actually looking at emotional information – the result of people's actions, thoughts and emotions.

Let me give you an example of why that is the case. If the stock market was a logical place, and there was no emotion involved in the share prices on the stock market, this is probably how the scenario would work.

For this example, I will use IBM. I am sure you have heard of this company before. Of course, this is not a real example about IBM; it is just an illustration for the sake of this example.

Imagine that IBM opens its books and produces accounts this month that show us IBM is worth $10 billion.

That is not the true price for IBM, but let's just say that it is true, again, for the sake of this example.

Also imagine the issued share capital of IBM is $10 billion shares.

If IBM's value was written down in its accounts as $10 billion and everyone agreed that it was a very technically precise figure and correct, and they issued 10 billion shares, then each share would be worth one dollar each.

If everyone agreed on that valuation and no emotion was involved and we were working on pure logic, the share price on the stock market of one dollar per share would not change. The only thing that would make it change would be if something fundamental changed in what had come through on those issued accounts. In the logical world, the share would have a real, tangible value.

If you think about it, it sounds very logical and maybe you think that is the way the stock market is.

It is natural to think about the stock market as logical because it is all about finance, numbers and business. However, to really understand the market, you need to reference human nature and the 'herd instinct' I discussed in Chapter Two.

What price can you charge for any product?

The answer is, whatever people are prepared to pay for it!

If I am a father who has promised to buy his son a particular toy for his birthday and had forgotten about it at the last minute, I could be faced with a price-altering situation and a heightened level of emotion and desire. I can run around town, from toy store to toy store, and after visiting 10 shops who have all sold out of the particular toy that I promised my boy, I have a completely different perspective on what the toy is now worth.

The example I give above is exactly what happened in the dot.com bubble in the 1980s. People paid much more than a stock was worth because they had to get their hands on the latest 'new thing'. Everyone (the herd) wanted a piece of the Internet craze.

Price action (price movement) is *the* single most important item on a trading chart. The price of stock changes all the time. If you study any stock in the market, it would be very, very, rare that a stock price would remain constant even for a day.

It does not stay the same all day because that is not the reality of how the stock market works. There is more to how the stock market works than looking at a logical value of how much a company is worth. That is only the starting point of a share price on the stock market when the stocks are originally floated.

I have shared some extreme examples above to drive the point home. The reality is much calmer movements in price much of the time. There is clearly emotion behind what actually happens day-in and day-out. The reason price analysis is so important is because you need to learn to read this emotional behavior behind the stock price movement.

Stock price moves because people have a different view on what the stock price might be worth in the future. Some people think it might be worth less in the future, and others think it might be worth more in the future. When more people think it might be worth more in the future, then more people are buying than selling, and the stock price goes up.

At the other end of this, when more people think it might worth less in the future, then more people are selling rather than buying, so obviously, the stock price goes down. That is what drives the market.

Luckily, reading price action is easy to learn and execute, especially with the simple technology now available.

Below you can see an example of a stock chart.

Stock Chart

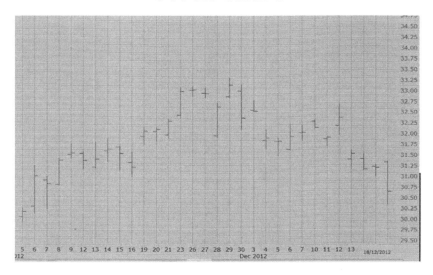

If you look briefly at this chart you can see that there are some bars on the chart.

If you would like to see the chart in full color, please see the Book Bonus webpage at: www.The-Cashflow-Trader.com/BookBonus.

You can also see that there are some dates along the bottom of the chart, the most recent date being at the very right-hand side of the chart.

The chart on the previous page is a daily chart. This simply means that this chart is giving us the price information for a single day in the stock's life cycle.

The market is open Monday through Friday. Weekends are not shown on the chart. There are also several bank holidays, so those bank holidays and weekends will not be on the chart. The chart shows only the days that the market is open and, again, the dates are along the bottom of the chart.

The price range of the stock is on the right-hand side of the chart. This is fairly typical for trading charts anywhere, but in this book I am going to use a tool called *Free Stock Charts* to illustrate what is going on with the stock.

All charting software will always try and give you the price range as it is relevant to the stock you are currently looking at.

The vertical trading bar that is nearest to the right-hand side of the chart is always the bar that you need to take the most notice of. This is what is tells you the price for today.

Pricing On Stock Charts

Now that you understand how to read a stock chart, let's look at pricing on the chart in detail and, in particular, at each individual bar on the chart and what it tells us.

Take a moment to study the diagram on the following page.

Reading Charts

OHLC Bars (Open High Low Close)

Look at the bar on the left first. This is a bar on a day when the price of the stock went up. On a colored chart, this would be green because that is the traditional color when the stock being discussed has gone up during the day.

What do the sections of this bar tell you?

First of all, it tells you the open price of the stock. This is marked by the small horizontal line on the left-hand side. There is also the longer vertical bar in the middle, which tells you the range of prices during the day.

As the prices and stock move up and down during the day, it will be marked within that bar. Then, when the market closes, the closing price will be marked by the small horizontal bar on the right-hand side.

The bars in the middle show the ranges during the day. Obviously, the highest points of the bar tells us the highest price that stock has reached during that particular day. The very bottom of the middle bar tells you the lowest price that the stock reached during the day.

The right-hand side bar shows you an example of the stock going down on a given day, which is traditionally marked by a red bar on a colored chart.

On the right side, the mark on the left tells you the opening price of that stock on any given day. The price movement during the day is marked by the middle vertical line, and then the closing price of the day is marked by the horizontal bar on the right-hand side.

The two trading bars that you have just looked at are called 'Open High-Low-Close Bars', which is not a catchy name, but I think you can see why they are called that.

Stock Analysis

Every investor wants to be able to read a chart. The basic task in the stock market for most investors and traders is to look back at evidence about the particular stock you are interested in and try to predict what will happen in the future based on the evidence you uncover.

There are, however, different types of analysis you can perform in the market to find out what might potentially be happening with your stock. Let's take a look at these.

Fundamental Analysis

The first way you can look at a stock is called fundamental analysis. Fundamental analysis is a forecast discipline based on the study of financial information and attributes of a company's management and competitive position.

Therefore, fundamental analysis is basically looking at a very long-term overview of where you think the company is going. It is also looking at attributes that are going to affect its performance in future years. This forecasting discipline looks at things much like management structure; a company's order book and contracts, their market position and things that affect their effectiveness as a business. All of these things and more can influence the growth and profitability of a company, which in turn, affects the long-term value of the company and its share price.

For fundamental analysis, think about it being used primarily for long-term 'buy and hold' situations.

Technical Analysis

If you compare what I have just illustrated above to technical analysis, then technical analysis is a forecasting discipline that is based on the study of past market data, primarily price data and volume data.

Technical analysis does not actually look at the company itself. Instead, it looks for patterns of how the price data of the stock has moved, and how the volume data of that stock has moved in the past.

Let me explain what I mean when I discuss price patterns. Human emotion is a repeatable cycle. That is, humans tend to behave in the very same way to situations over and over again. I refer you back to Chapter Two where we talked about how people behaved in the market when a stock is deemed "under bought" or "over bought."

Just think about this for a moment. As a human being, there are certain things that frustrate or annoy you in everyday life. Now as logical as you'd like to think you may be or as calm and controlled as you like to think you may be, I bet that when a certain thing occurs in your life, it usually gets a very predictable reaction.

Just like the herd in the buffalo example, humans also react in very predictable ways.

This doesn't mean that if a pattern in a stock price movement over time is repeated that the end result will be the same, but to most people who look at technical analysis, it does mean that the same result is likely.

Price and Volume Data

Price data is the market quoted value of the stock, which you can read straight from your stock chart.

Volume data is the amount of the stock (how many shares) that is bought and sold within the time interval being looked at.

For instance, if a trader is looking at a one-hour chart and studying the change of price within that last hour, volume data can show how strong the move was and let them know what is likely to happen in the next hour.

For example, if twice as many people are buying the stock from 2:00 PM to 3:00 PM as were buying it between 1:00 PM and 2:00 PM, then we may conclude that even more people will buy it from 3:00 PM to 4:00 PM and drive the price even higher. This is a very simplistic example but I hope you get the general idea.

Technical analysis is concerned with how the price has moved and how strong the move was.

Traditionally, technical analysis was used by people who were looking at short-term traits. Fundamental analysis was used by people who were looking within long-term traits.

I use the word "traditionally" because these two fields used to be very separate fields of analysis. People used to focus on one or the other. They would never touch the other because they didn't believe in it. But nowadays, I know traders and investors who use a combination of both. Which one they rely on the most depends on what strategy they are implementing.

The importance is in understanding that there are two different approaches to analysis and both have their benefits. Therefore, don't be driven into just one camp.

Do not focus on "I only care about technical analysis" or "I only care about fundamental analysis" because both have their uses and will play a vital part in your trading and investing future.

As you see more strategies through your trading research, you will see that some strategies will lean more towards technical analysis, and others will lean more towards fundamental analysis.

Chapter Eight - Options Basics

Why Do People Trade Options?

In this chapter I cover options basics so you have an understanding of the options market in general. I share what people do in the options market, why it is there, how people interact with each other in it and what people are looking to do while they are there. The goal of this chapter is for you to understand what generally happens in the options market rather than what you are specifically going to do.

Once you have this knowledge under your belt, it will be time to move onto understanding my own preferred low-time, low-risk approach to the options trading market.

Options Terminology

Before I tell you how we make money from options, first I will break down the terminology we are going to use.

What Is An Option?

An option is the right to buy 100 shares of stock at a specified fixed price and by a specified date in the future.

All you need to remember in the options market is that you can buy options *and* you can sell options.

Just like we can buy and sell shares; we can also buy and sell options on those shares.

There are two types of options available in the market. There are 'Call Options' and there are 'Put Options'.

What Is A Call Option?

A Call Option contract, is an option acquired by a buyer or granted by a seller to

buy 100 shares of stock at a fixed price within a specified time period. The key about a call option is that it is about buying the stock.

The call buyer has the right to buy 100 shares and will generally believe that the share price will rise because that's where they are going to make some money on their option. If the share price rises, the option is going to be worth more. That is what they are interested in.

Both parties have a different belief. The option seller believes the share price will remain the same or fall. The option buyer believes that the stock will rise and go up in value and that is where they will make their money. This is a general belief in the market around this option tool.

These beliefs will become clearer as you move through the chapter and go through some examples.

What is a Put Option?

A Put Option contract is an option acquired by a buyer or granted by a seller to **sell** 100 shares of stock at a fixed price within a specific time period.

The key about a put option is that it is about selling the stock.

A put option buyer has the right to sell 100 shares and will generally believe that the share price is due to fall because if it does, the put option price will rise as the share falls because with a put option, value increases as the share falls.

Both parties have a different belief.

The option seller believes the share price will remain the same or rise. The option buyer believes that the stock will fall and the option will go up in value and that is where they will make their money. This is the general belief in the market around this option tool.

Again, these beliefs will become clearer as we move through the chapter and go through some examples.

What Are The Written Elements of an Option?

Below is a written example for a single option.

MSFT CALL JUN14 29 0.53

I will guide you through this example by explaining what each element means throughout the example.

MSFT CALL JUN14 29 0.53

MSFT - The Share Symbol

What Is A Share?

A share is a unit of ownership that represents an equal proportion of a company's capital. Each share has a share symbol or stock symbol. In this case, we're going to talk about Microsoft shares. MSFT is the share symbol for Microsoft. What you see, therefore, is an option on Microsoft shares.

MSFT **CALL** JUN14 29 0.53

CALL – The Type of Option

What are the Different Types of Options?

As I mentioned above, there are two types of options we can use in the market. One is a Call Option and the other one is a Put Option.

A call option is an option acquired by a buyer or granted by a seller to **buy** 100 shares of stock at a fixed price within a specific time period.

A put option is an option acquired by a buyer or granted by a seller to **sell** 100 shares of stock at a fixed price within a specific time period.

In short, the difference between a 'Call' and a 'Put' is that

- a CALL OPTION is all about the right to BUY A STOCK
- a PUT OPTION is all about the right to SELL A STOCK

MSFT CALL **JUN14** 29 0.53

JUN14 – Expiry Date

Understanding Options Expiry

Throughout this book, I describe how to use monthly options to your benefit. To understand, there are two expiry dates you need to be aware of.

The expiration month – Every option traded has an expiration month that is listed as part of the options details. For example: JUN14. This option expires in the month of JUNE, 2014. Always make sure you trade an option with the correct expiration date for the strategy you are using.

The expiration date – The third Friday of the expiration month is the last trading date for an option.

The first thing you will recognize, just from reading the definition, is that a monthly option doesn't expire at the very end of the month. A monthly option actually expires at close of the business day on the third Friday of the month.

The third Friday of the month is the last time you can trade an option. Then on the Saturday, the day following that Friday, is when any action relevant to the expiration of those options takes place, when the market is closed.

MSFT CALL JUN14 **29** 0.53

29 – The Strike Price

What is the Strike Price?

A strike price is the price written into an option contract at which the option is exercisable.

Do you remember the original definition of an option? The stock can be bought or sold in the future at a specified price. Well, the strike price is that specified price. In the example shown, the strike price is $29.

The strike price is usually quoted in whole dollars or half dollars.

So there could be strike a price at $29.50, $28, or $28.50. In this example, the strike price is at the price of $29.

MSFT CALL JUN14 29 **0.53**

What is the Option Premium?

The option premium is the price that needs to be paid per share to buy that option.

The premium is the amount of money you collect when you sell an option contract, or the amount you pay when you buy one.

The premium is quoted as amount per share. However, the main thing to remember about option premiums is options are bought and sold in *contracts* or lots of 100 shares.

Option Contract

You may only buy or sell options in contracts. Each contract grants an option for 100 shares. In other words, 1 Contract = 100 shares.

If the option price is $0.53 a share, then the premium for one contract is actually $53 (100 times $0.53).

Calculating the Option Price

An option price is made up of two elements. One is its 'Intrinsic Value' and the other is its 'Time Value'.

The intrinsic value is the difference between the actual share price and the strike price. The rest of the value of the option price is the time value. Time value reduces as we get near expiration. For example:

Stock Price = $29.00
Option Price (Strike Price $28.00) quoted in the market $1.50

The intrinsic value of the above would be $1.00, the difference between the actual share price of $29.00 and the strike price of $28.00.

The time value would be $0.50. This is the total option price, minus the intrinsic value $1.50 - $1.00.

How Time Value Works

With each option purchase, there is a limited time for the stock to move to the strike price. Time value deteriorates as we get closer to options expiry date.

Think of the time value of an option as a block of ice. Then think about an electric heater blowing at it and slowly melting the ice away. Over time, the melting of the ice gets quicker and quicker. This is a way to think of the time value in an option deteriorating.

Why Would People Use Options In The Market Then?

The short answer is because options provide leverage.

Here is another example. Imagine that a stock is currently quoted in the market at $29.

Let's say someone buys a call option on that stock for $1.50 (the option premium) that has a strike price of $28.

The person who is buying that option has a right to buy that stock at $28 even though it is $29 in the market (at any time until the option expiry date).

In terms of intrinsic value for the above example, the value of the option is $1.

Intrinsic value is the difference between the strike price and the stock price.

What is left of the option's price is obviously the time value, the $0.50 that is left over because there are the two components that make up the total option price of $1.50.

Here is where the leverage comes in.

What happens when the stock goes up in price?

Let's say the stock now moves to $29.50. What happens to our option price?

Well, the intrinsic value has gone up, hasn't it?

We still have a right to buy the stock at $28, but now the stock is worth $29.50 and the difference between $28 and $29.50 is $1.50.

Let's assume our time value is still the same, $0.50. This means that the total price of the option has moved from $1.50 to $2.00.

Percentage Return

Let's also look at the percentage return on the stock on the stock price movement.

$29.00 to $29.50

Percentage return on investment is investment return (your $0.50 increase) divided by your investment capital; the $29.00 you originally paid for the stock, multiplied by 100.

$0.50 / $29.00 = 0.0172 x 100 = 1.72%

That is an example of the unleveraged return of normal trading.

Now let's look at the percentage return on the option price movement.

Percentage return on your options investment is investment return (your $0.50 increase in the option price) divided by your investment capital; the $1.50 you originally paid for the option, multiplied by 100.

$0.50 / $1.50 = 0.33333 x 100 = 33.33%

The option price has increased by 33.3%.

I hope this example helps you to see how much leverage you can get out of trading options in the market.

You have a unique opportunity to make money quickly if your stock rises quickly. If you have done your research and the stock rises quickly, and you have an option on that stock, then you can make a lot of money in a very short space of time. However, there is a huge amount of risk involved because once you get to options expiration day, the option is worth zero. That's correct, absolutely nothing.

This means that if the option doesn't move in the time that you have it available for, you can lose everything that you have invested.

So if the option goes up by 33% how would you make sure you retained that profit?

The answer is that you can actually sell the option to someone else before the expiration. Remember, you can buy and sell the options themselves.

This is how money is made trading in and out of options.

In other words, in this example you just take the 33.3% profit on the movement in the price of the option. You have no intention of actually purchasing the stock that you have the option to buy.

Your intention from the beginning is to trade in and out of that option for profit.

Many people target making large percentages by gambling on quick stock movements in the options market, but they take large risks in doing so. Clearly, the opportunity for quick profit is there, but so is the opportunity for large losses.

As good as this sounds – and I admit, it does sound fantastic – there are very clear drawbacks to this way of leveraged trading.

Remember at the beginning of the book that leverage was one of our five obstacles to successful trading.

Chapter Nine - Using Options To Our Advantage Without Leverage Dangers

If you want to avoid the dangers of leverage, can you still make money in the options market?

The answer is, yes you can. You can make consistent money during most months with very little activity. In fact, it won't take you more than 5 minutes a day.

Do you see where the opportunity comes in options trading? It is in getting time value on your side.

Keep the valuable analogy of the ice block in your mind. The people who purchase options have the ice block and the heater is against it and the ice is melting with each passing moment. If they do not get a movement in price to their advantage before the ice melts, then all of that time value is gone and they have lost the money they have invested. That is what is happening to the person who bought an option.

In other words, time is against the person who buys an option.

Then who does have time value on their side? The answer is, the seller of the option.

Let me explain it another way, by using an insurance company as a part of this next analogy.

The Insurance Company

I want you to imagine household insurance. The insurance company takes a premium from you to insure you against an event that may or may not happen. In the case of this example, the event is a theft. You will be expected to pay a premium, each and every month, in case of possible theft of your home.

Is your house definitely going to get burglarized?

No. The possibility exists that you will never experience a theft in your home. But you pay the monthly premium nonetheless because you know that "in the event of a burglary, I will be covered."

The actual theft of your home may or may not happen, and certainly, you hope that it won't. The actual chance of it happening is quite small, but it does exist. So you trade a small amount of theft insurance payments just in case of the event that you do get robbed. In that case, you will get a check to cover your damages, usually a much bigger check than the premiums you pay each month. That is how the insurance company works.

Is the insurance company happy to collect your payment every month?

Yes, of course they are. They are happy to collect the small premium even though they may have to write a much larger check to you in the future. The insurance company collects premiums from many people and therefore are taking enough money to cover their liabilities for those who have been burglarized, and they still have enough left over to make a profit at the end of each year.

They provide you with a service and you are happy to pay the premium, even though a theft may never occur over the course of your policy term. In the event a theft does occur, you know you will get much more money than you paid for the premium.

If you think about the insurance analogy and you compare it to the options market, the person who buys an option is the person paying the insurance premium. They may get a lot more in return but it's not very likely. The person selling the options premium is acting like the insurance company, and they are getting regular money every single month. Doing this, they may eventually have to take on the liability that the option sold for. That is what is happening.

When you take out the insurance, the insurance company is the one with time value on their side. Why is this? Because the insurance policy is an annual policy. It has an expiry date. If you insured your house against theft, you are only covered until the end of the year. If the year had ended and you had not paid another premium, then you have no right after that to ask the insurance company for any recompense even if you were to suffer a burglary.

If you never make a claim within the year, what happens to all the premiums that you have paid to the insurance company? Do you get them back? Of course you don't. The policy has lapsed or expired and they keep the premiums you have paid.

Monthly vs. Annual (Time Value)

Now I ask you to consider one further item of interest in this insurance company scenario. Let's say you just want the insurance coverage for one month. Perhaps you are going on vacation and you just want that extra protection while you are gone and your home will be vacant. If you call the insurance company and ask for a quote, how much would you pay? Do you expect that it will be one-twelfth of the annual premium? If your insurance is $600 annually, would you expect to pay $50 for the month of coverage?

Absolutely not.

If you want short-term insurance, the premium changes. It is always more than one-twelfth of what you would pay annually. This is because it is a limited time insurance. The insurance company is not getting consistent business from you so they charge more.

How can you become like the insurance company in the options market? You are going to sell options. The important thing to remember is that is *all* you are going to do.

No buying options, just selling them. Because when you sell options, you get consistent money every single month and time is working for you. As soon as you sell that option, the time portion of the premium is decaying and the likelihood of the option being exercised is decreasing daily.

There is another really important point here about the option premium you receive. Once you have sold the option, that money is yours to keep whatever happens to the value of the stock.

Chances are very good that what the buyer is expecting to happen will not happen. Selling options is important because it is very low risk, as long as you are not leveraged and you get time value on your side.

The other important point from the insurance example above is that monthly premiums are better than annual premiums, so not only are we going to sell options, but we are going to sell monthly options, which will increase our earnings.

I am going to give you an example of the starter option strategy that will show you exactly how this works, so hold on to your hat and get ready to see the result of everything you have been learning about.

Chapter Ten - Killer Strategy – Selling The Call

In Chapter One we discussed the first obstacle to successful trading which was the 'buy and hold' mentality, and I showed you that 'buy and hold' had brought us up to think that we could only make money in one of three market directions.

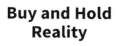

Buy and Hold Reality

Stock Profit

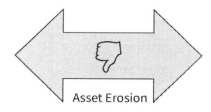

Asset Erosion

Stock Loss

I also shared how a specific group of property investors were doing much more

Note: Shorting A Stock

When I explain this in the classroom, some people tell me this is not true because you can 'short' a stock in the market and this process makes money when a stock goes down. This is true, shorting a stock, if you get it right, will make money when the market goes down. However, if you short a stock and the market goes in the opposite direction (up), then you will lose money. So shorting still only makes money in one direction.

than 'buy and hold' and were making money in all three directions.

Remember, they make monthly income from their base asset all of the time by receiving rental profit every month.

The arrows in the diagram show the direction of the price of the base asset - regardless of the direction though, they make a profitable monthly income.

Cashflow Trader Method

Asset Increase & Cashflow Profit

Cashflow Profit

Cashflow Profit

Your stock market opportunity is to do the same.

To make money every month, whether your stock market goes up, down or sideways.

You're going to love *The Cashflow Trader method*.

Cashflow Trader Method

Asset Increase & Cashflow Profit

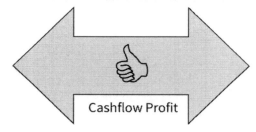

Cashflow Profit

Cashflow Profit

The arrows in the diagram show the direction of the price of the base asset - regardless of the direction though, they make a profitable monthly income.

So how do you apply this property principle to the stock market?

The answer is, of course, that you use stock market options.

Let me show you how to use options to achieve this amazing result.

I will guide you through a flow chart of the process that you can put into practice to achieve monthly income by selling call options in the stock market on a base asset or stock that you are happy to keep long term and invest in.

Step One - Buy Stock

Step one is to buy your stock. There is one key rule you need to apply when selecting the stock that you are going to buy. This is to know that you would be happy to hold onto it for the long term.

Covered Call Selling Process

Step 1

Buy Stock

Here are your criteria for your stock:

1. You are confident that it will not go to zero.
2. That it has potential for long-term growth.
3. You do not want its price movement to be static. It has to be a stock that moves a lot in price. (In other words, is it volatile enough to mean you can trade options on it with a good level of premium income?)

Step Two - Sell An Option On The Stock

Step two is that you sell an option to someone else which gives them the right to buy your stock from you at a price that you fix.

Covered Call Selling Process

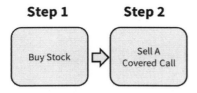

You are going to sell them a monthly option. That means that they only have this right to buy stock from you for this option month only. (Remember the option month expires on the third Friday of the month.) We sell monthly options because over the year it gives us a better return than using longer-term options.

Now here's the really clever bit. As the person who is selling the option, you get to choose the strike price at which the other person can buy your stock from you.

The price that you fix for the strike price is a price higher than you paid for your stock. That is, you are giving somebody else the right to buy your stock from you at a price higher than what you paid for it! This means that if they exercise their option, their right to buy the stock from you, you will get an automatic profit.

In return for the option that you are selling to them, they are going to pay you some money (the option premium).

When you sell this option, the person who bought your option pays this money for the option immediately. Depending on which broker you use, the money is usually in your trading account the very next day!

Now you haven't finished the whole process of this options trading strategy yet, and already you've made your money. That money is yours to keep whatever happens next.

Are you getting excited yet?

Step Three – Options Expiry

Now let's move to step three. Because this is a monthly option it has an expiry date and that expiry date is always less than a month away from when we sold the option. What happens next in this strategy depends upon where the price of the stock is on expiry date.

Covered Call Selling Process

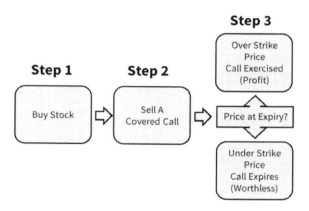

If the price of the stock at expiry date is above the price that you fixed to sell the stock at, then the person who bought the option automatically purchases the stock from you. If this happens, you will make a profit on your stock because you have automatically sold it for a higher price than you paid for it. In addition to this, remember, you were paid some money when you sold the option, so you have made money in two places.

If, however, at the expiry date the price of the stock is below the price you fixed when you originally sold the option, the person who bought the option will not buy the stock because it hasn't reached the required price. In this case, because the option had a fixed period of time, it will expire and you will no longer be under any obligation to the person who bought the option.

Step Four – Your Profit and Actions for Next Month

So if the stock price is above the strike price, you have made money in two places. In addition, if the stock price stays below that price and doesn't get to the strike price, you have been paid some money for the option and you have made some money during the month. So in this case, you keep the stock and you keep the money that has been paid to you (the option premium).

Covered Call Selling Process

If you keep the stock, and you are no longer under any obligation because the monthly option has expired, you are now free to go back to step two of the process and sell an option to somebody else for the following month.

You can repeat this process month after month and make income each month.

Covered Call Selling Process

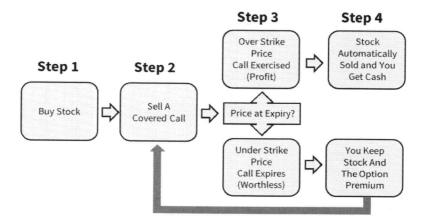

What if the price had risen on expiry above the fixed strike price and the stock has been purchased from you? Then obviously, you would be back into cash and you could now go and repeat the process with the same stock again, or you could choose another stock and apply the same process to that.

Why Is This Such A Killer Strategy?

I am going to give some financial examples in a moment, but before we do that I want to share why this is such a killer strategy. I'm sure that you haven't failed to notice that there is something truly amazing about this process that we have just gone through and the amazing thing is this...

Whatever happens on the option expiry date, you will make a profit!

Let me repeat that. Whatever happens on the expiry date, you will make a profit! How amazing is that?

You will either sell your stock for profit and collect an option premium, or you will keep the stock and make a profit by collecting an option premium on the option you have sold.

The point here is, if you buy a base stock that you are happy to keep for a long time, you can make money every month whether the stock goes up in price, the price stays the same, or the stock goes down in price.

Doesn't that sound much better than just buying and holding the stock? You now have a strategy that gives you cash flow time after time, month after month, and more importantly, it gives it to you consistently.

How Much Money Can I Make?

Let's look at the same strategy when we put some numbers to this process.

This is what you are going to do. You are going to buy shares in the stock. You are then going to sell an option, giving someone else the right to buy 100 shares from you at a price higher than you paid for them.

The important thing here is that when you sell one option, it gives the other person the right to buy 100 shares of your stock. One option contract controls 100 shares of stock. In this example:

> You buy one hundred shares in Microsoft at $28.74 on May 20th 2014.

You then sell the following monthly option to someone else.

> MSFT CALL JUN14 29 0.53

Remember the following:

> MSFT: is the stock symbol for Microsoft.
> CALL: is the type of option you are selling.
> JUN14: is the month that the option expires.
> 29: is our fixed 'strike' price.
> 0.53: (cents) is the price you are going to be paid per share for that option.

When you sell this option, because the option contract is for one hundred shares, you will receive $53.

It is important to note the percentage returns on this strategy. If I show someone this strategy, they might be tempted to say "$53 dollars, that's not much. Is it worth the effort?" But that would be failing to understand what you can achieve as you add more funds to this strategy.

Look at what can be achieved with a more substantial investment and then you can look at how you will progress over time with this strategy.

Investment Example

What happens when you invest £25,000 pounds in this strategy using the same trading information I've just discussed?

How many Microsoft shares could you buy?

> £25,000 pounds is $38,932 dollars. If we divide $38,932 by $28.74 we can see that you can buy 1,354 shares.

Each options contract you sell is for 100 shares, so you can sell 13 contracts.

> (1354 divide by 100 = 13.54)

For each contract you would receive $53 dollars. If you sold 13 contracts you would receive $689.

> (13 x $53)

Now take a look at your percentage return on investment (ROI).

> Percentage return on investment = investment return (your money in),divided by the money that you invested (your money out), and then you multiply that by 100 to get your percentage return.

So you divide $689 (investment return) by the $38,932 (your investment) that you used to buy the stock.

> $689 / $38,932 = 0.01769

Then you multiply the result by 100.

> 0.01769 x 100 = 1.76%

Now remember that is your _monthly_ return. That is pretty fantastic!

That is the money you make if your stock doesn't go up in value.

If your stock went up in value past the strike price, in addition to the money we worked out above (which you would make at step two), you would get the additional money that you made on the profit of selling your stock for a higher price than you paid for it at step 3/4.

Using this example, on 1300 shares you would make quite a profitable sale. You bought each share at $28.74 and you would sell them at the strike price $29 dollars. You would therefore make a profit of $0.26 per share.

$0.26 x 1300 = $338

That represents another $338.

Let's work out your percentage return on investment if that happened.

Your return is now $338 + $689 (share profit + premium profit) = $1027. That means that your return divided by investment is now

$1027 / $38,932 = 0.0263

0.0263 x 100 = 2.63%

Awesome, right?

What I have shared here is an absolutely killer trading strategy. It is a winning strategy and one that produces consistent monthly returns.

You can make 1.5 to 2% per month on average even if your stock doesn't go up in value. If your stock does go up in value, you can make even more. Also, don't forget that if the stock falls in value, you still keep making money - between 1.5 and 2% per month until such time as the stock recovers.

Let me assure you that I am just touching the surface here in demonstrating the power of this strategy. There are plenty of stocks to choose from which will work well with this option strategy.

Brilliant, if I do say so myself!

I call it 'brilliant' because when you are making 1.5 to 2% per month, it amounts to over 20% per year.

You will honestly not mind if the stock takes years to recover or never recovers because you are still making that monthly cash flow and you can and will build wealth from that monthly cash flow.

In other words, you do not need your stock to go up to build your wealth.

What are the major 'pluses' of the strategy?

- You can use the same stock repeatedly so you are not researching new stocks all of the time, like most traders do.
- You sell monthly options, so you only have to do one trade each month.
- You make consistent income. There may be one or two months out of the twelve-month calendar year where you could not get the right amount of money for the options so you would not sell it that month, but in those months, you would not be losing money.
- The worst that could happen to you in this strategy, when executed correctly, is you get zero percent in a month.
- You only need to spend five minutes a day checking the price of the option so you can sell the option when the premium is at an acceptable level to you.

In short, this is the awesome strategy that delivers on the subtitle of this book.

In just five minutes a day, while looking calmly at the market without any additional monthly expense on fancy trading software, and sleeping soundly at night after you place your trade. This option strategy will deliver 1.5 to 2% per month on average. That is well over 20% per year compounded. And that is just using one simple option strategy.

I hope you now understand and have seen the power of options and that you can see why I use them as my trading tool of choice.

Keeping The Risk Low

Note that in this strategy you already own the stock. If someone who bought the option from you wanted to exercise their right under this option and buy the stock from you, then you have the stock and you are happy to deliver it.

This is a very important part of this approach to trading.

Yes, it does require you to have money to invest, but it also means that you have kept your risk to a minimum when you sell the option.

When you sell a call like this, it is called a 'covered' call because you have the obligation that you are selling already covered.

Should you ever sell a call without having the stock to back up your obligation, it is called a 'naked' call.

We all know it's not good to be caught naked! So take heed and be sure to always sell a 'covered' call.

The covered call is the world's easiest option strategy. I recommend that you grab hold of it and make it your own.

A Word on Strike Prices

It is important to realize that you are in control of the strike price you choose for the option. Depending on the strike price you choose, the option premium will change.

To illustrate, there is a list of all the strike prices that are available on a share at a brokerage and all the premiums that are relevant to those strike prices on the following page. You can look down the list and you can choose any of the strike prices.

The strike prices are in the left-hand column. The other column of note is the bid column. This is the price that people are bidding in the market right now to buy and option on that share, with that strike price.

A great concern most people have is will they be able to find people to buy the option and pay them the money every month. The reality is that in the U.S. Markets (where I trade) there are hundreds and thousands of people for each strike price on suitable stocks.

I love it every time I look at this screen at *Options Xpress*. I think to myself, "Look at all of those people waiting to give me money. Isn't this strategy fantastic!"

It is like walking past a long line of people who are holding out handfuls of money and they are asking you to take it.

▲ Strike ▼	Last	Chg	Bid
July 2014			
10.00	8.71	0	8.95
11.00	8.55	0	7.80
12.00	7.47	0	7.75
12.50	0	0	7.15
13.00	7.10	0	7.20
13.50	0	0	6.70
14.00	6.28	0	6.20
14.50	4.83	0	5.70
15.00	5.30	0	5.20
15.50	3.55	0	4.70
16.00	4.35	0	4.20
16.50	3.82	0	3.70
17.00	3.30	0	3.25
17.50	2.81	0	2.70
18.00	2.30	0	2.27
18.50	1.78	0	1.72
19.00	1.31	0	1.29
19.50	0.86	0	0.83
20.00	0.47	0	0.45
20.50	0.21	0	0.21
21.00	0.10	0	0.09

Now don't get me wrong, they *are* getting great value from me.

After all, if the stock price went up significantly, I wouldn't get that all of that profit. I would get $0.26 profit per share. The shares would then transfer to them for $29 dollars, and they would be the ones making the rest of the profit.

What you are doing is exchanging the promise of a rare up-lift in the stock every now and again, which is what they prefer, for a regular amount of money every month and a more modest gain when the stock goes up.

In my opinion, regular and consistent money wins every time.

Here is what I recommend to you. Instead of waiting for all of the bigger returns, what you do with options is say, "I don't care about the promise of maybe getting the occasional 10%; what I am quite happy with is the certainty of 1.5-2% a month and I'll let those regular returns build my wealth and be happy building it that way."

Always remember, "A bird in the hand is worth two in the bush."

Each time you sell an option, you have the profit in your hand immediately. The person you sold it to has got two birds "in the bush." They have a potential profit. But that's all it is – potential –and there are many months when they get nothing for their efforts.

I know this touches on something that you've probably been wondering…

Why Would They Buy The Option I'm Selling?

If you've been asking yourself this question, you are not alone.

People often ask me the following questions:

- "Why would they buy an option in the first place?"
- "Why would they buy an option to buy your stock from you for more than it is worth right now?"
- "Why wouldn't they just go straight to the market and buy the stock for the lower price that it is now?"

All of the above are very good questions. The answer is straightforward and I am sure you have guessed it by now. It is because they think the stock is going to go even higher.

No matter what is going on in the market, some will speculate that a stock will go down, and others will speculate that it is going to go up.

That, in essence, is why people purchase options in the market and although they think it is going to go up, they can't be certain.

Options allow them to control the price they can buy the stock at in the event it goes up. However, if the stock doesn't go up and they are wrong, they merely lose the small amount of money they have paid for the option.

Make sense?

We have already covered the second reason that people buy options when we were discussing options leverage. They are looking to buy the option, wait while it goes up in price, and then sell it to someone else who wants to actually purchase the stock at that price.

These are the two most common reasons and I am sure there are many more. The market is huge. There are many players and as long as there are people buying, you don't really need to worry or care about why.

These people have a different strategy than you, that's all.

Do not try to speculate on their speculation. Just understand that they have a *different* trading strategy than the one you have. It is that simple.

The goal for you is to have clarity in this regard.

The reason people do what they do in the market is because of their trading plan and strategy. Your focus is on your own strategy and adhering to it, no matter what is going on around you.

Chapter Eleven - Buying Stock BMV (Below Market Value)

In the previous chapter, I showed you how you can make monthly income by selling monthly options on a stock that you already own.

In this chapter I am going to show you how you can make an option trade when you don't have stock that will do one of two things.

> 1) It will enable you to buy a stock you would like to own below its current market value or
> 2) It will make you a return monthly on you cash.

As before, I will walk you through the put selling process through diagrams.

Step One - Choose A Stock

Choose a stock that you would like to own.

You need to know that you would be happy to hold onto it for the long term.

Put Selling Process

Step 1

Choose
Stock You
Are Happy
To Own

Step Two - Sell A Put Option

Step two is to sell a monthly put option to another investor. That gives the other investor the right to sell their stock to you at **a strike price that is lower than the current market price of the stock**.

Put Selling Process

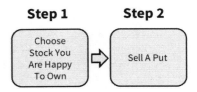

Step 1

Choose Stock You Are Happy To Own

Step 2

Sell A Put

They only have the right to sell their stock to you for this option month only. Remember that the option month expires on the third Friday of the month. You sell monthly options over the course of a year because it gives you better returns than using longer-term options.

The clever bit is that again, you have chosen the strike price. You have told them that they can only sell the stock to you if it falls in value. This guarantees that if it does get sold to you, it will be below the price that it currently is in the market right now!

Perfect!

In return for the option that you are selling to them, they are going to pay you some money (the option premium).

When you sell this option, the person who buys your option pays you money for the option immediately. Yes, it is just like in the call selling process. Again, the money is usually in your trading account the very next day!

Step Three – Options Expiry

Because this is a monthly option it has an expiry date that is always less than a month away from when you sold the option. What happens next depends where the price of the stock is on expiry date.

Put Selling Process

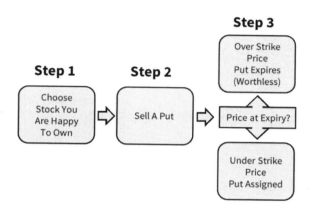

If the price of the stock at expiry date is below the price that you fixed, then the person who bought the option automatically sells you the stock at the strike price.

Remember that you need to have put the money aside for this purchase. You always need to back the option you are selling with the required resources to take action. On a covered call, this was you holding 100 shares for every option contract you sold. With a put, this is you having the money in your account to buy 100 shares at the agreed strike price for every contract you sell.

Step Four – Your Profit and Actions for Next Month

If this happens, you will have bought the stock cheaper than it was when you first sold the option. In addition to this, remember that you were paid some money when you sold the option, so you have made money in two places.

Put Selling Process

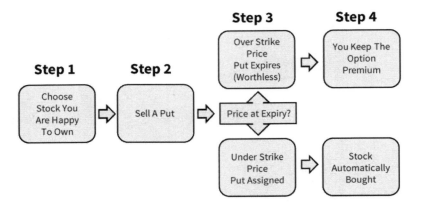

If however, at the expiry date, the price of the stock is above the price you fixed when you originally sold the option, then the person who bought the option will not sell their stock to you. In this case, because the option had a fixed period of time, it will expire and you will no longer be under any obligation to the person who bought the option. If the stock did not fall in value past the 'strike' price, then you will still have cash in your account and you can repeat the process next month.

Put Selling Process

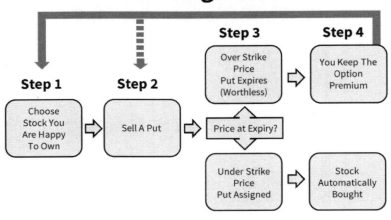

Why Would Someone Buy a Put Option?

As I walk you through using actual numbers, I will use the insurance company as an example once again to explain how this works.

An insurance company makes a lot of money by protecting people against something they fear will happen. Keep that in mind while going through this next options example.

Someone in the market has a share that is worth $20. They are worried that it is going to go to fall in value to less than $18. They do not want it to go lower than $18. Instead of selling the stock (which they would do if they were sure it was going to fall), they keep the stock and buy themselves some insurance.

The insurance they buy is the put option that you are willing to sell them.

Having decided that you are happy to buy the same share, if it drops in value to $18, you sell them a put option in the options market and say to them, "If your stock goes down to $18, you can sell your stock to me at that price."

If their stock goes down to $18, they can sell their stock to you.

Remember, they have the right to do this, but not the obligation. But you do have the obligation, which is why you need to have money ready to buy the stock.

Basically, you are being the insurance company for the other person.

But do you think the stock goes down every month?

Of course not. Most of the time, you collect the "insurance premium" that they are paying and you do not have to take the stock.

This is a good thing.

You want to be the insurance company.

Chapter Twelve - 5 Minutes A Day

I hope that I have simplified the process for you in a way that you now feel comfortable and confident about trading and that you have a familiarity with the stock option process.

The next thing to understand is that this process should not take you more than 5 minutes a day.

First of all, I would like to draw to your attention that while you may not have heard of trading stock options before, you have probably encountered options in your daily life on a number of occasions. This options principle happens in people's lives with regularity.

Options are a Familiar Process

To illustrate this I have chosen an example most people can relate to – the purchase of a car.

Option 1 - You can buy a car for cash with a deposit to hold the car.

In this example, you agree to purchase a car for a certain amount. You want to go and raise the funds to buy the car and you need some time. You put down a deposit to hold the car and you write up an agreement that you will pay the balance at a specific time.

If you agreed to purchase the car at $30,000 and you put a $2,500 down payment, then the balance left on the car would be $27,500.

The $2,500 is a deposit to hold the car while you go to raise funds. It holds the car for you. In this example, the $2,500 is the option premium you have paid.

You have gone to the showroom, you have picked your car and the salesman has written the agreement and you have given him a check for the $2,500. You now have a specified amount of time (the option term) to go and raise the rest of the money.

What happens if you decide you no longer want the car during that period of time?

Typically, you lose the deposit (the premium you paid), because as soon as you paid it over, it was theirs. The deposit was to 'hold the car' for you for a specific amount of time. They did their part. They were holding that car for you. They could argue that while it was sitting on the lot with a 'sold' sign on it, other willing buyers wanted to purchase it and they had to turn them away.

Do they have a right to keep your deposit?

Yes, they do. The deposit is the option premium.

You agreed to a specified price and arrangement. What happens if a few days after you leave the lot, you see the very same car, fully loaded with the extra luxury options for the same price you agreed to pay for the basic version?

You want the fully loaded car, right? After all, the stereo is better, it has a sunroof and heated leather seats. In addition, this dealer is offering a special where you also get a free GPS, as well as a $200 gasoline card!

You do some math and you realize that this car has a value of $4,200 more than the previous car you paid a $2,500 deposit on.

If you walked away from the first deal, you would lose your $2,500 deposit, but because the value of the second car is $4,200 more, then you would still gain $1,700 in value. Losing the deposit, but gaining the extras with this new car, you still get a benefit.

In this case, there is an obvious benefit in letting the option lapse on the first car.

The person who was holding it for you also got a benefit. They still have the car that they can sell and they made $2,500 worth of benefit for agreeing to hold it for a few days.

Option 2 - You can buy the car on a lease option.

You may not have heard the phrase 'lease option' before, but I guarantee you will recognize the process I will describe to you.

In this scenario, you pay an amount up front on the $30,000 car.

Let's say you will pay $2,500 down.

The payment balance left on the car is $27,500. Your agreement is to lease the car for 24 months at $250 per month. At the end of the 24-month-term, you would have paid a further $6,000 for the option of leasing it. ($250 x 24).

In the case of a lease option, both the deposit and these monthly fees are 'the option premium' you have paid for the control of the asset (the car) over the 24 months (the option term).

You haven't paid nearly enough over the term to own the car outright but at the end of the fixed term, you have the choice to either purchase the car by paying the agreed upon balance price (the 'strike' price), or give the car back and let the option to own the car expire.

If you no longer want the car you don't have to buy it. However, if you would like to own it, you must pay the remaining agreed balance (the 'strike' price) and the car is yours.

Option 3 – Property.

Let me offer yet another example of an option from the world of real estate property to help give you more clarity and understanding of this.

There is a property that is for sale, but for whatever reason, it is not selling.

As a property investor, you find it, knowing that eventually the property is going to go up.

Since the seller wants to sell their property but cannot sell it right now, you suggest to him that you take it over for him for the next five years (the term) with an option to buy in five years.

You will make the payments on that property and pay all of the expenses (these payments are the option premium). The owner can go ahead and move away.

The seller's asking price is $100,000. You mutually agree on a purchase price of $110,000 (strike price) with the option because you know the price will easily go up above that in five years' time.

The seller is happy because the property is, in all respects, sold and now he can move on. You are happy because you get the option to purchase the property and can hold that with the monthly payments you are making.

The seller is the person with the asset and he can make something out of it. You have a price that you agreed upon and a transaction will happen in the future that works for you, so you are happy.

If you are familiar with just one of the above examples, then you are already familiar with what an option is. You just had not heard the terminology in regards to stocks or trading before.

Checking Options Premium Prices

There are two things that will excite you.

> Checking the options premium prices is simple.
> Checking options premium prices is quick.

The way I do it is that I look at the strike price that I want to sell at on the left of the chart.

I then go to the bid price to the right of it, and that is the premium I will collect per share when I select to sell that option.

It really couldn't be any easier.

Refer to the chart on the following page and use the chart to understand what I just described above.

▲ Strike ▼	Last	Chg	Bid
July 2014			
10.00	8.71	0	8.95
11.00	8.55	0	7.80
12.00	7.47	0	7.75
12.50	0	0	7.15
13.00	7.10	0	7.20
13.50	0	0	6.70
14.00	6.28	0	6.20
14.50	4.83	0	5.70
15.00	5.30	0	5.20
15.50	3.55	0	4.70
16.00	4.35	0	4.20
16.50	3.82	0	3.70
17.00	3.30	0	3.25
17.50	2.81	0	2.70
18.00	2.30	0	2.27
18.50	1.78	0	1.72
19.00	1.31	0	1.29
19.50	0.86	0	0.83
20.00	0.47	0	0.45
20.50	0.21	0	0.21
21.00	0.10	0	0.09

Please Note: *Shown on the chart is the 'gross' premium you will collect. Your broker will have a charge and you will get slightly less 'net'. Please see your brokers' terms and conditions.*

Market Liquidity Makes Transactions Fast

You can trade very quickly because you are in such a liquid market.

Options are not available on all stocks but are available on many.

The U.S. markets have the largest number of optionable trading stocks and, therefore, that is the place to go if you want to trade options. I want you to have stock liquidity. So you will want to get to somewhere where you can trade in only five minutes a day.

If you want to sell an option, you need someone to respond to that sale and buy immediately, so you are not spending time waiting and hanging around. You do not want to wait a half an hour for somebody to decide if they are going to buy something from you. You want to sell it to them in *seconds* so that you may go and do whatever it is that you want to do.

It is very important that every time you want to do a transaction there is someone there to take the other side of the transaction, immediately. In order to do that, you must be in the biggest ocean with the most fish.

People from all around the world are trading in the U.S. market. I reside in the U.K. but I trade in the U.S. market. The most liquid market in the world is the U.S. market, and that is why people all over the world trade there through the Internet.

That is exactly what we are after, more opportunity!

The more people who are trading in an options market, the better. You have liquidity of those options, so you can buy and sell options very quickly, and that is exactly what you need to do. You need to sell options quickly and without fuss.

Also, the U.S. market has monthly tradable options, which give us 12 opportunities a year to use the strategies that I have outlined.

Finally, the number of people transacting trades in that market is huge. Every time I sell an option in that market, the transaction happens in a second. It is really great to see. I literally click 'sell', and one second later the option has been sold.

It is this convenience that makes five minutes a day possible.

Chapter Thirteen - The Base Stock

In this section, you will learn more about the base stock you will be using for your strategy and how to select it.

The very best stocks to use for these strategies are ones that have the following three key criteria:

1) Intrinsic value
2) Produce premiums of at least 1.5-2% monthly
3) Channel within a defined range

We will discuss the concept of intrinsic value later in this chapter under the heading "What Happens If The Base Stock Goes Down?" and we have already discussed how to calculate return on investment, so you can evaluate the available option premiums.

Choose a Channeling Stock

The definition of a channeling stock is a stock that moves within a repeatable range and gives you the opportunity to buy and sell the same stock over and over again.

In the diagram below, you can see the stock moving between a lower price and a higher price. It goes from one price point to a higher price point, and then it moves back down, to a lower price point, and then back up to a higher price point again. It keeps repeating the pattern.

Channeling

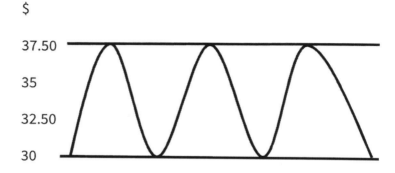

So Why Are Channelling Stocks So Great?

In the diagram on the previous page, the straight line going horizontally across at the low price point (30) is the line to watch as the stock price moves. Know this line as your line of support. It helps to think of this line as a <u>floor</u>.

The straight line going horizontally across above the high price point (37.50) is the line to watch. Know this as your line of resistance. It helps to think of this line as the <u>ceiling</u>.

The numbers on the left show the value of the stock in dollars.

To minimize your risk, always locate a stock that channels within a clearly visible repeatable range.

Finding a channeling stock does not mean that the stock will never break through the resistance (the ceiling), or never break through the support (the floor). What it does mean is that the stock has some predictability about it in recent times.

The other great thing about a channel is that you know that you will get decent option premiums.

Remind yourself why people will buy options from you. They will buy them if they see a likelihood of the stock price moving in the next month. They need the stock price to move in order to fulfill the two main reasons that people buy options:

1) The stock price moving in the right will mean an increase in the option price and they can then sell that option onto someone else at a profit, or
2) The stock price will move past the strike price that is agreed and they will be able to buy the stock at the price they want.

If a stock is consistently moving between two price points (between an obvious floor and ceiling), then it is likely that more people will want to buy options.

What this means is that you will have people lining up to buy options from you.

The diagram on the previous page is a very simple diagram of a channel. Stock channels do not have to have sideways movements. If you find a stock that channels, you will also find that even when it is moving down it will channel, as you can see in the next diagram.

Channeling

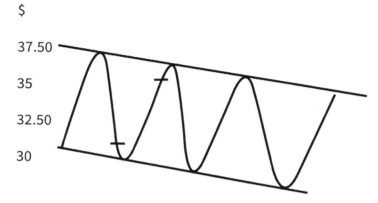

And when it is going up in price, it will still channel.

Channeling

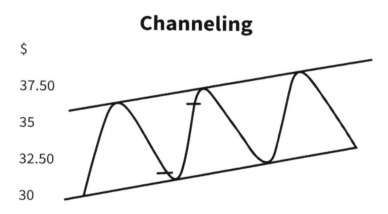

Remember what I mentioned earlier, you can make money whatever market the direction is going in.

What Happens if the Underlying Stock Goes Down?

I have to take this opportunity to mention something of importance. When I am teaching this, the number one question I get asked is, "What happens if the underlying stock goes down?"

Answer 1 – You Accept That Risk Already

If you elect to stay in the 'buy and hold' world, then know that your stock may go down. It has the potential to go down a lot. But you have already accepted the risk that the stock can go down in value. Everyone has. They don't like it, but they have accepted the risk anyway.

If you adopt my new strategy, surely it is an improvement on what you already have.

What you already have is the risk without the monthly income. At least with the strategy that I have demonstrated, you have monthly income to offset the downside fall in your stock.

If you don't do this strategy and you remain in the 'buy and hold' world, then you have that risk and you are not making monthly income. Whereas with this strategy, you potentially still have that risk, but with the monthly income.

Answer 2 – The Key Is Using a Base Stock That Has Intrinsic Value

Remember our property investors and their income strategy? There is one important attribute that property has that makes the people who own it very positive about its ability to recover its monetary value when the price of property falls. This attribute is intrinsic value.

Most people in the world are pretty happy that their property has a really good intrinsic value that it can't go below, even if the property burns down and that intrinsic value is the land that it's built on.

As long as the property has been selected in a place where land is scarce, and there is a high demand for that land, this will hold true. The property has good solid intrinsic value.

So research and seek out the stocks that have solid intrinsic value. When you do this, your trust in this options process will be solid.

In the United States market, there are hundreds of such stocks available.

Answer 3 – Don't Sell If The Stock Goes Down in Value.

People have a fear about the underlying stock going down because in 'buy and hold' world, which many people are in, they then wonder what happens when the stock goes down? The answer is that people instantly become fearful that the stock will go to zero. Fearing this, they sell very quickly and take a loss, whatever that loss may be. This is how the thought patterns run in 'buy and hold' world. This fear occurs to many people at the same time, much like the herd and it causes a mass hysteria.

Oftentimes, the loss is very significant.

People forget they have a choice.

You will choose not to go down that road rapidly when that fear kicks in because your emotions will not be tied to the trade.

Remember, you are safe because your strategy takes a stock and then makes a monthly income of it.

You can only take a loss if you sell your stock for less than you bought it for. If you choose your stock wisely, you don't need to fear it going to zero. If you apply the intrinsic value rule above, you will be confident that going to zero isn't a possibility and, therefore, you can keep the stock and sell monthly options on it and keep making consistent income, regardless of the value.

Remind yourself that this is what the smart group of property investors do. They are not fearful and panicked when the value of their property goes down. They are confident and know that the property has intrinsic value so they hold onto it and keep building their wealth from monthly 'rental' profits.

If it works for them, why wouldn't it work for you?

Answer 4 – Return Of Investment Removes Your Risk

Throughout this book, when you have been looking at the return you can make from investment strategies, I have been demonstrating to you the return on investment of each strategy. This is the common way that all investments are measured.

At this time, I would also like to introduce you to a new concept for measuring the effectiveness of an investment over time. One of the secrets of wealth building is this, to take measure.

Measure the results of all investing strategies over time by looking at how long it takes to get all your initial investment money back.

Measure return *of* investment rather than return *on* investment.

On the following page is an example of how this option strategy can perform when you measure things in this way.

What if you bought some shares worth $20 and using the call option selling strategy, you achieved a $0.50 premium on average each month from selling the monthly options. I have included some tables which show that if you count your monthly return as a return of your initial investment, this effectively reduces the cost of your investment each month by $0.50.

This process is called reducing our net cost basis and you can see how it works in the chart provided.

50% Return of Initial Investment

Month	Premium Collected	Net Cost Basis
1	0.50	19.50
2	0.50	19.00
3	0.50	18.50
4	0.50	18.00
5	0.50	17.50
6	0.50	17.00
7	0.50	16.50
8	0.50	16.00
9	0.50	15.50
10	0.50	15.00
11	0.50	14.50
12	0.50	14.00
13	0.50	13.50
14	0.50	13.00
15	0.50	12.50
16	0.50	12.00
17	0.50	11.50
18	0.50	11.00
19	0.50	10.50
20	0.50	10.00

Table 1

You can see from Table 1 that after 20 months, you have half of your original investment money back.

100% Return of Initial Investment

Month	Premium Collected	Net Cost Basis
21	0.50	9.50
22	0.50	9.00
23	0.50	8.50
24	0.50	8.00
25	0.50	7.50
26	0.50	7.00
27	0.50	6.50
28	0.50	6.00
29	0.50	5.50
30	0.50	5.00
31	0.50	4.50
32	0.50	4.00
33	0.50	3.50
34	0.50	3.00
35	0.50	2.50
36	0.50	2.00
37	0.50	1.50
38	0.50	1.00
39	0.50	0.50
40	0.50	0.00

Table 2

You can see from Table 2 that after a further 20 months (40 months in total), you have all of your original investment money back.

PART THREE

Part Three shows you how to develop the correct mindset to trading. In every field of life where you see success, the key thing behind it all is having the correct mindset. This, followed closely by the correct preparation, and then, the correct actions.

Chapter Fourteen - Demonstrating The Trading Challenge

The Trading Mindset of A Successful Trader

As you look into successful trading, you will discover that your mindset and your attitude towards trading is one of the things that contributes the most to your becoming a successful trader.

In order to understand why mindset is so key to trading, I will share an example that demonstrates the problem very clearly. This is an example that I use consistently in *The Cashflow Trader Program*.

Imagine yourself on 'another' trading program and you have been given a strategy. After you have been shown all the details of the strategy, you are shown that the strategy is successful on 7 out of 10 occasions. This means that if you perform this strategy, for every 10 trades you do, on average 7 will make you money, and 3 will lose you money.

After being taught the strategy, how would you feel leaving that trading course? Chances are that you would feel highly confident that you are going to have some trading success because 7 out of 10 is not bad. You have learned carefully, you understand the strategy, and you are determined to implement it well.

Let's begin.

After waiting for the correct trading signal to come, you will carefully - after checking everything - put on your first trade.

Bingo! Your first trade is successful and you make money.

Now you're ready to do your second trade.

Let me ask you a question. How confident do you feel now about putting on your second trade?

At this juncture, I am sure you will answer the same as most people, and that is that you're feeling very confident. You have a trading strategy that is right 7 out of 10 times and you just applied the strategy and it worked. Why wouldn't you be confident?

You take your second trade and Bingo, again! Your second trade makes you money! Congratulations!

How confident do you feel now about taking your third trade?

You're most likely feeling quite confident now, aren't you?

You take your third trade and, Yes! It's a success once more and you make some more money!

At this point, you are three trades into the new system and every trade so far has been a success!

You are most likely feeling quite pleased with yourself now. I'm sure you would agree that you are pleased because you've executed a strategy well three times in a row and the statistics of your quoted system are adding up really well.

How confident do you feel about taking your fourth trade?

If you are anything like everybody else who's been asked this question, you will now be saying that you feel even more confident about the fourth trade, having seen things work so well, time and time again. I'm that sure, like most people, you would have no hesitation in taking the fourth trade and applying the strategy perfectly.

Now let's come to the crunch!

Let's revisit our first trade again. You will still do the exact same strategy. You have been told it works 7 times out of 10. You prepare yourself, just like before, and you take your first trade.

However, on this occasion, the first trade loses you money.

I'm going to ask you the same question. How confident do you feel now about taking your second trade?

I leave you to answer that question to yourself and let's move on to your second trade.

You take your second trade and that one loses you money as well.

You have now had 2 trades that have lost you money and you haven't made any money at all!

How confident do you feel now about taking the third trade?
If you are like most people, you are feeling a bit nervous about taking your third trade even though you logically know that you are still within the parameters of what you've been told. The strategy consistently brings 7 out of 10 wins and 3 out of 10 losses. Knowing this, I bet you will still be nervous about taking this third trade.

Reluctantly, you take your third trade and even though you follow the strategy perfectly, this trade too, is a loss.

Now ask yourself how you would be feeling if this was the first trading strategy that you had learned and were putting into practice?

My guess is that you are beginning to have some strong doubts about whether the strategy was all it was cracked up to be! It's likely you feel cheated and disillusioned at this point. You just lost your first 3 trades on a system that you were feeling very confident about.

If I asked you now about how you feel taking the fourth trade, after losing the first 3, I'm sure that you would be feeling very edgy and nervous about taking that next trade. You would feel very uncomfortable about putting your hard-earned cash on the line, again.

Am I right?

Most people who experience this have the feeling of a huge rock in the pit of their stomach just from reading this.

The key message here is that you completely changed emotion in the two scenarios even though no real money has been spent. When you were experiencing wins, your belief was different about the strategy you were using then, when you were experiencing losses.

You must learn to take both of the above scenarios the same way emotionally. In other words, whether you win or lose, you have to feel the same. But most people do not because of the fear of loss.

The fear of loss triggers all sorts of emotions and they will react based on those emotions, no matter what the strategy statistics show.

Look again at the statistic we have been given. On average, 7 trades out of 10 will bring favorable results. The other 3 out of the 10 will not.

You can see that in the case of the losing example (3 out of 10 losses) you really have no logical reason for feeling suspicious about the strategy at all. Three losses out of 10 is still within the statistic of 7 out of 10 just as you had been told. Yet the fact remains that you are suspicious, you are nervous, and you consider the strategy, and probably trading in general, a threat to your hard-earned cash.

So what can you conclude from this exercise I've just put you through?

Here is the critical point. When you are trading, the mind doesn't deal in logic. In this exercise, you have no real money on the line at all and yet your mind still told you that one scenario was better than the other. Your mind couldn't stop interpreting what was a very logical situation in a very emotional way.

In short, the emotion of the situation got the better of you.

I'd also like to point out that if you actually had some real money on the line in this scenario, you probably would have gotten even more nervous than you did just thinking about it!

The real problem here is that the more nervous about the situation in trading you are, the more you will think about it. The more you place yourself in such a position, the more you will respond to fear and imagine scenario after scenario in which you're going to lose money, rather than make it.

Therefore, to be a successful trader you need to be very clear on the mindset required. You must also be disciplined in keeping the right mindset. Developing the correct mindset is imperative to being a successful trader.

Now that you understand why mindset is so important, let's get into some specific things that will help you.

Chapter Fifteen - Commit to Unconscious Competence

A concept I want to discuss with regard to mindset is the concept of unconscious competence and the act of committing to unconscious competence. In order to demonstrate what this actually means, I'm going to take you through the key stages of learning and talk about the concept of how conscious we are of what we're doing. Then I will delve into unconscious competence in some more detail. I will use the example of learning how to drive a car to demonstrate the key stages of learning.

Stage 1 – Unconscious Incompetence

The first key stage of learning is unconscious incompetence, and what this means is that we don't know what we don't know.

With regard to learning to drive, imagine that you are 6 or 7 years old and you're in the back of your parents' car. As they are driving along, it's likely that they are listening to music or speaking to you every now and again. You may notice that they are also speaking to each other. It appears as if they don't have a care in the world and it most likely does not occur to you, at age 6 or 7, that it may actually be difficult to learn to drive or that it may involve a complex process.

This unawareness is the first stage of learning and it is unconscious incompetence. You don't know it's hard to learn to drive. You just see the result and that is that the car is moving.

Commit To Unconscious Competence

> **Unconscious Incompetence**

Stage 2 – Conscious Incompetence

Over time, you become aware of the fact that you can't drive. You realize that the car does not just go on its own and that they actually have something to do with it. This awareness about driving probably kicks in when you are 15 or 16 and eager to learn to drive. At that point, you have reached a state of conscious incompetence. It is when you know what you don't know.

You become aware of what you can't do because you're suddenly sitting in the car with your first driving instructor and they are saying, "Alright, you need to put one foot here, you need to put another foot there, you need to have your hand on the gear stick ready to change, you need to look into the mirror, you need to check your blind spot…" and so on. They are going through a long list of things you were never aware of before.

To top it off, you have this powerful engine in front of the car that you know you can do some real danger with if you don't get it right. Suddenly, you become very aware that you're incompetent at driving.

Commit To Unconscious Competence

Stage 3 – Conscious Competence

As you go through the learning process and somebody teaches you about driving, you eventually get to a stage where you're taking your driving test and you're going to be measured about your competency and skill. If you have learned correctly, you will walk away with your first driver's license.

That third stage is conscious competence. It's when you are aware of being competent and the numerous things you actually need to do to be competent at driving. When you take the driving test, you have to think carefully and concentrate. You most likely won't listen to music or speak to anyone. You have to really concentrate and fixate on what you are doing. You have to have focus. So you are competent, but only when you are very conscious of what you are actually doing.

Commit To Unconscious Competence

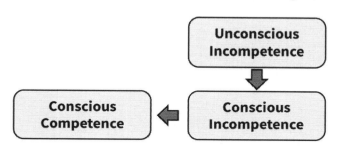

Stage 4 – Unconscious Competence

Finally, you get to the state where you know what to do and you don't really need to think about it. In this driving example, this is long after you have passed your driver's test and you've been driving for some time.

Driving has become second nature and you don't consciously have to think about the basics of it anymore. Your foot naturally finds the brake pedal.

At this point, you are just like your parents were when you were 6 or 7 years old and you realize that you're driving down the road, listening to music and chatting away. To the observer, you appear not to be concentrating on what you are doing.

Of course, if someone stepped out in front of the vehicle, you would immediately slam on the brakes. This would happen because you've become unconsciously competent.

You are competent and you don't even have to think about it anymore. You can multi-task and do other things at the same time.

Commit To Unconscious Competence

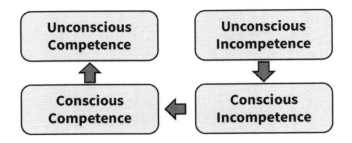

How We Apply The Principle of Committing to Unconscious Competence

It's important to mention that how you learned to drive is different than how you learn other things. You don't actually go through all those four key stages of learning with everything you learn as a human being. Because of this, I would like to share another example.

Think about being in a room that hasn't got a light on.

Now imagine getting up and going over to turn the light switch on.

When you go and turn on the light switch, you don't stand there thinking to yourself, "Now hang on! I'm not going to push this switch until somebody explains how electricity is made, how the electricity gets here and whether it's safe and question that all of the correct safety procedures have been followed. Only then, when I am sure that nothing bad will happen to me, will I hit the switch."

You don't go through all those thoughts, nor do you measure it against your learning and make sure you know everything about it before you turn the light switch on.

So why don't you do that?

You don't do that because you learned about the effect of turning on a light switch in a different way. You learned how to turn on the light by watching others turn the light on. You saw that when they flipped the switch, 99.9 times out of 100 the light came on. You got used to the fact that's what you do if you want to turn the light on. You just flick that switch and it happens. Presto! Lights on!

What you have done in that example is that you have committed to unconscious competence. You are competent without even thinking about it. You're competent of using electricity and adding light to a room without even knowing all the processes about how the electricity got there, how it's manufactured, whether it's safe or not. You just want the light on, and so you turn it on.

Your Learning Choices

So whenever you are faced with learning something new in life, there are two paths that you can take. The 'learning to drive' approach is going through all four steps in great detail and taking years to master something, or you can head for the short cut. You can learn by modeling the approach of someone else who has gone before you. This is what you did in the light switch example. You modeled or copied the behavior of someone else who had gone before you and if you do what they did, you get the same result.

Unconscious Competence in Trading

It is this state of unconscious competence that I want you to commit to in trading.

As you read and learn about trading, then obviously you are going to get some of your questions answered. But what I really want you to be aware of is that you don't need to know every single detail behind a strategy in order to execute it perfectly. In fact, the more you know about it may actually hinder your trading capabilities!

To put this into proper context, imagine when you're fearful of doing something. Perhaps it's something that is new to you.

Which way will make it easier to execute? If you actually think of all the stuff that could go wrong or if, instead, you focus on the fact that the other people are doing just fine and you've seen their results?

They are doing something that works for them and they are getting the result from a specific process. Are you going to focus on questioning the process or will you execute with faith, trusting that you will get a similar result?

If you can get into a mindset of unconscious incompetence, you will be much happier learning about trading, and eventually, actually trading. Be prepared to commit to it and not worry about every little detail.

Fear is a very dangerous thing. If you worry about every little detail and you learn too much about trading too fast, I can predict what will happen to you—you will find yourself in a state of 'analysis paralysis'.

I'm sure that you've heard that phrase before. What it means is that you go over so many different things, and you are faced with so many pieces of information about the decision that you are due to make, that you get to a point where you have difficulty taking any action at all. You freeze and the opportunities pass.

If you freeze due to overanalyzing things, then you cannot take action in trading, you make no money and you do not succeed.

Of course, you need to get the 'modelling' or 'copying' right. You wouldn't turn on a light switch with wet hands for instance! The important point when committing to unconscious competence is not the detail behind why something works the way it does, it is in applying the process exactly.

What I recommend you do is to commit to unconscious competence.

Make sure you understand that if you follow a process and execute it, doing what you are told, you're actually going to be okay, and you will be a successful trader.

Chapter Sixteen - The Belief Cycle

The Belief Cycle – Negative Mindset

The next concept concerning trading mindset that I will discuss is the concept of belief and how the power of your beliefs influences the results you get. Belief and confidence are very important aspects of being a successful trader. In order to demonstrate the belief cycle, I'm going to use the example of learning to play the piano.

Belief

Imagine that you are interested in learning to play the piano. You think it will be nice to sit at the piano on Christmas and play a few tunes with the entire family sitting all around. This idea appeals to you and you think it would be nice to be able to sit down and play a tune every now and again. But here's the thing; you are not positive that you will definitely succeed, and this is a key fact.

I want you to note the difference between liking the idea of doing something versus being unstoppable. The belief I have just outlined is far from being unstoppable. You are in the "Well, it might be quite nice to learn to play piano" belief.

Negative Mindset

> **Belief**

Action

The next stage of this cycle is to take actions based on your belief. So if you have the belief that it would be 'nice to learn to play the piano' but you are not totally committed to doing it, you are not going to go out and buy a piano (they are not cheap) because you're thinking, "That might be a waste of money if it doesn't work out." So you decide to try playing the piano at a less committed level.

What you are willing to do at this stage is go onto Amazon and buy one of those little inexpensive electronic keyboards for $100-200. The ones where you press a key and out comes one of those cheesy drum patterns. Of course, it has some piano sounds on it, which are not really particularly great, but you can get away with playing, 'tickling in the ivories' on it. So that is what you do. You may even be wondering what kind of results you will get from this half-hearted action, but it is the action you will take, nonetheless. This is because you are not fully committed.

Negative Mindset

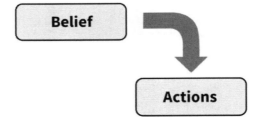

Leverage

The next stage, in addition to your initial actions, is how you leverage your actions and what you do to improve your actions. Two of the things that you can leverage the most are time and money, and this is what you do. In terms of time, you spend some time to learn to play the piano, and in terms of money, you try to make the experience better and to make the experience happen for yourself.

If you are not unstoppable and you just think it might be a good idea, do you think you will practice every single day, or do you think that you will go into your room and practice every now and again, when the mood hits you? Probably the latter.

So how will we use our money to leverage our learning? If you are not as committed as you should be, you will be thinking, "I'm not quite sure if it's going to work out but I do want to have a good go at it." You are not going to go out and pay a piano teacher. Instead, you are going to go back to Amazon again and you are going to get one of those *Learn To Play Piano In Five Days* style of books.

Every now and again, you will practice in your spare room with your little keyboard and your *Learn To Play Piano In Five Days* book. That is the extent of what you are going to do to further your ambition of playing the piano.

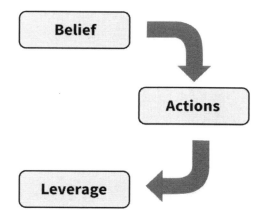

Results

Off the back of that belief, the actions you take and the leverage of those actions, you will get some results. But what kind of results?

If that is your attitude and that is how you commit yourself, practicing every now and again, not getting the proper equipment, substituting a book for a real teacher, what sort of results do you think you are going to get?

I am sure your thoughts are similar to mine. The results you would get are not going to be very good, and you are absolutely correct. The results are not going to be very good if that is also the kind of attitude you have when starting out.

Negative Mindset

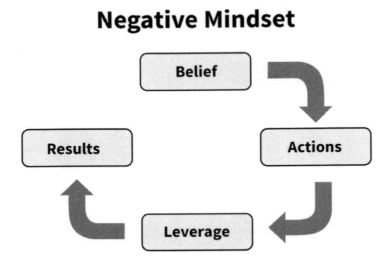

Here is the most important takeaway from the process I have just outlined.

You can clearly see why a poor belief is not going to prepare you to do anything in life. Whether it be trading or learning to play the piano, a poor belief will not assist you.

The important thing is that when you get those results, in this case poor results, you go back into your belief system and the poor result actually serves to reinforce your beliefs. Meaning that the results you get actively reinforce those poor beliefs.

You belief system then says, "That was a great idea to learn to play the piano, but it isn't working out too well. I didn't think it would." You might go around the cycle a couple more times, practicing the piano, but eventually your poor results are going to make your belief say, "This isn't working; I'm going to stop."

What you'll most likely do then is take your little electronic keyboard and your *Learn To Play Piano In Five Days* book, get them together and wander over to a cupboard you have at home. There you will open the door and put them away and never think about them again. I'm sure you have one of those spaces at home that houses the things that you've given up on in the past? That is what happens when you have a poor belief about something. Everything else, all the actions you take, all the leverage you take, and the results you get all come off the back of your belief.

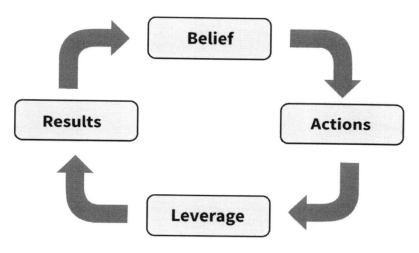

Negative Mindset

A poor belief leads to low levels of action and leverage, and then poor result. Poor results reinforce the poor belief, making it deteriorate over time until you finally just give up.

The Belief Cycle – Positive Mindset

Now let's look at this belief cycle and what it can achieve if we adopt a positive belief from the start. What would the piano learning cycle look like when you are actually committed to learning to play the piano?

Belief

You say, "I want to be a piano player and nothing's going to stop me. I know loads of people who play the piano. I can see it can be done. I've seen lots of people playing the piano. I'm going to apply myself to learn and I'm not stopping until I can play." That is a powerful strong belief, isn't it?

Positive Mindset

┌─────────────────────┐
│   **Belief**   │
└─────────────────────┘

Action

Let's consider the actions you are likely to take when you have that belief. Will you buy a piano? Yes, you absolutely will because you are going to learn to play the piano and you view it as a lifetime skill you are learning. You cannot think of anything more important than having the piano and having the pleasure of playing the piano because that is what you want to do. You go right out and buy yourself a $7,000 piano without a second thought. You are committed.

Positive Mindset

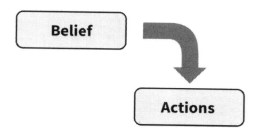

Leverage

You want to succeed and to do the best thing, so when it comes to leverage, what are you going do to with your time? Are you going to spend a lot of time practicing? Of course you are! You are going to spend all of your free time practicing because you want to reach your goal as quickly as possible. You want the pleasure of playing the piano and you are determined to succeed.

Will you hire a music teacher or a coach?

Absolutely. You will hire a music teacher or a coach because you know that doing so will get you to your goal even faster. You know that you will progress and get to where you want to be quicker, so you value the input a music teacher or coach will bring.

Positive Mindset

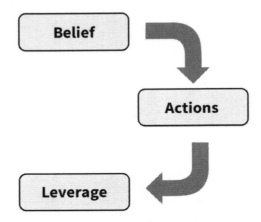

Results

So if you bought the piano, you practice as much as you should, you hired a piano teacher to help you along and teach you all the things you don't know, what sort of results are you going to get?

You are going to get good at playing the piano even as you are just learning, even as you are starting out. You are going to look at your results and say, "Hey, this is working. I'm starting to learn a few tunes and I'm putting my hands in the right places more consistently. My coordination is improving, as is my playing speed. Things are really working for me."

If you have enough reasons to believe, you say, "It's really working for me," and this becomes a self-fulfilling prophecy.

Positive Mindset

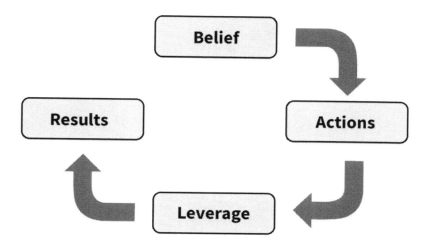

So you go around the cycle again and you take the necessary actions again. You give it time and you keep going back to your music teacher. You follow instruction well and you do all the things your teacher tells you, and then you get even better results.

Positive Mindset

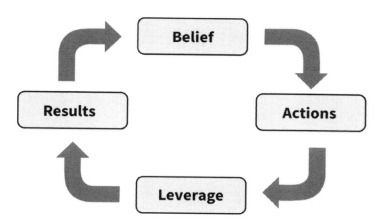

When you are committed, you will practice every day, every chance you get.

The more times you take positive action and get improved results, the stronger your belief becomes and your positive attitude to learning the piano increases. You just keep going around the belief cycle reinforcing, reinforcing and reinforcing. And it's really helping you move closer to your goal of being proficient at playing the piano.

The Power of Mindset

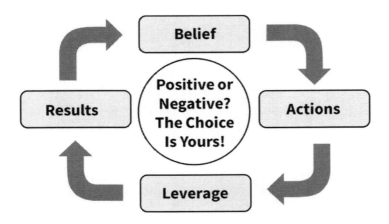

Can you see how important belief is to being successful at something now? Obviously, belief is hugely important in trading.

Help With Your Belief In Trading

The greatest help is to have a clear understanding of the basics and to find the right mentor. You have to see evidence of results—something you can model and copy. A result you can see, that you believe in and will pursue. Make sure your mentor takes you through everything you need to be successful, not just the right equipment and tools, but the proper mindset, too.

To reiterate: belief is a very important factor in your trading success. One of the phrases I use most with my students is TRUST THE PROCESS. The concept of belief that I've just shared and the previous concept of committing to unconscious competence is all about *trusting the process*.

Chapter Seventeen - Achieving The Calm, Logical Approach

Trading Should Be Boring!

Yes, you read that correctly. Trading should be boring.

Doesn't that have a nice ring to it?

"Hmmm," you are thinking to yourself, "I'm really excited now!"

Not.

The reason I say this is because I want to remind you of the emotion that I spoke about earlier. You have to avoid getting too emotional.

The reason I say "trading should be boring" is because you will want to go through a very repeatable run-of-the-mill process. You never want to be punching the air when you have made a trade or when you have sold an option because that is not what trading is about. Remember, this is about the income. You can compare it to when you've been in a job for ten years and you get the same amount of money every month from your job. It's just payday.

Yes, it is nice to have a payday, but you don't go jumping up and down as if you won the lottery when you get to your paycheck. You know it is coming; it is a normal, regular occurrence. Just imagine how good your attitude is going to be toward trading if you just assume that you are regularly going to get a paycheck from your chosen strategy. You know it's going to be as regular as working because you have that much confidence in the system. You trust the process and it is coming to you in a run-of-the-mill way. That is how it should be.

That being said, be mindful that that should be your approach to trading.

Don't start trading for excitement. If you want to get that feeling of excitement about what you earn then I suggest you take some of the money that you get in from trading in your run-of-the-mill way and go and bet on a race horse with some of the money. Not all of it, obviously, but if you want some excitement, go do those kinds of things. Just do not get your excitement from trading or begin to associate emotions with your trading process.

Trading is not a place for excitement; trading is a place for calm and logical ways of doing things. You want each and every day you trade to be methodical.

Trust The Process

Develop absolute confidence in your chosen system. *'Trust the Process.'*

You need to get yourself to the point where you trust the process as quickly as possible. To do so, you must have absolute confidence in the system. When you have absolute confidence in the system, you will get to the point I just spoke of when I talked about trading being boring and where you view trading as just a payday.

Get Into The Flow

I understand it may sound strange, or a bit 'out there' for some, but there is an opportunity flow in life, and there is an opportunity flow from the stock market. All you have to do is put yourself in the path of that flow at the right times. Another way of looking at this is in the phrase 'fortune favors the prepared'.

The market is not something that needs to be conquered or beaten. It's not some big Goliath you need to take down. No, it's not like that at all. The market is just what it is and it is there all of the time.

Let me ask you another question. Before you begin trading a strategy, have there been others doing that same strategy before? During all of the time you were not trading and doing all those other things you have been doing for the last twenty years, have they gone through that trading process, day in, day out, for the last twenty years?

The answer is yes. I have been one of them. I have been trading and making money from trading for ten years, and there are others who have been doing it day in and day out for many more years than that.

All this time, the market has been there. All of these opportunities have been there. It is not something that just happens because you are discovering it now, and that you must 'go and conquer.' You simply need to make yourself available to the opportunities that the market presents and that is what I mean by getting into the flow.

Make Yourself Available to Opportunity

How do you make yourself available to the opportunities the market presents?

It's simple. All you need to do is follow the rules of your chosen strategy.

I have taught a number of trading strategies to *The Cashflow Trader Program* students and most of those strategies involve that they check for opportunities for just five minutes each day. A lot of the time the right opportunity only exists (or shows itself) once a month.

I have had students say to me, "I was looking day after day, five minutes a day, I was on there."

"I was doing my five minutes a day and after two weeks I still hadn't got a signal so I didn't look for a couple of days and then I went back…."

And guess what happened in those two days that they didn't look?"

Yes, you guessed it. There was a signal.

It was the only signal that month and they missed it. This means that they didn't make their money for that month.

That is a shame, isn't it?

When I think about this, I just do not understand. Why would you do that? You have worked to get yourself into trading and then you forgot to get into the flow and it cost you.

The market was there, giving you an opportunity, and you just refused to take it. Instead, you chose to close the door on it. It's almost as if someone was standing in front of you, holding out free money for the taking and you refused to take it! "No, I don't need any free money today!"

It would be crazy if someone offered you free money and you said, "Well, no, I won't take that today, thank you!"

Yet, that is exactly what you are doing each time you take yourself out of the flow. If you have learned a strategy and then you don't actually go and look at the market, ignoring the things that you have been taught, then what you are doing is having somebody hand you some free money and you are saying, "No thanks, I won't have any of that."

I stress this because it is madness! You are being crazy when you do that, so please maintain your focus and do exactly what you have learned. If you do, you will have so much fun with this.

Your results will be unbelievable if you just follow directions and do the work. So the take-away here is that you make yourself available to the opportunities that the market presents.

Chapter Eighteen - Avoiding Mistakes from Day One

Over the years I have seen so many friends and acquaintances start trading only to see them quickly fall by the wayside as they struggle for consistency. As I have been at pains to point out in this mindset section of the book, it is not just about a working strategy, it is about much more.

Let's have a look at the typical cycle of a trading beginner and discuss the implications.

Stage 1 – Planning and Great Discipline

What typically happens after someone learns a new strategy from a trading program is that they begin right away, full of enthusiasm. "This is fantastic!" They think, "I'll go home. I'll write my trading plan and I'll be ready to trade. I'll do everything I've been taught to do." So they do that and things start working great for them.

Stage 2 – They Make Money

They make money because they're doing what they've been shown. They make themselves available to the opportunities the market presents and they make money.

Stage 3 – They Take Risks and Break The Rules

After they've been trading successfully for a bit they start thinking, "Hey, look at me, I am a fantastic trader. I am absolutely rocking this. I'm brilliant at this stuff!"

At this point, they get over confident and once they get overconfident, and instead of accepting that the system works and they can make lots of money, they begin wondering what would happen if they made a simple little tweak to the strategy.

They begin asking themselves, "Will I get some more money this way?" and instead of testing these tweaks in their virtual account, they start testing them in their live account. Can you predict what happens?

Stage 4 – They take Heavy Losses to Their Trading Account

My recommendation is that they should stick to the strategy. If they are going to test anything it would be better to test it in their virtual account. But instead, they take risks based on their overconfidence and inexperience. They take risks based on their emotions. They are high at the moment, and they stop thinking. They break the trading rules that they have been taught.

What do you think happens when they take those risks and break those trading rules?

Usually, they start taking heavy losses in their trading account. Remember, if you must test anything new, test it in your virtual account first. Never in your actual account with real funds at stake.

Stage 5 – Quit! Enough Already! Or Restart The Cycle

At Stage 5 they either quit because those few bad trades have totally wiped out their account and they have no money left, or they actually start the cycle again.

The ones that start the cycle again know what they did. They think, "I became too overconfident. I broke the rules. What I should do now is go back to planning and being disciplined again and I should just make money." They are right on. That is exactly where they should be. They never should have deviated from the strategy in the first place. They should have been disciplined and planned and made money in the way they were taught.

But guess what they do next?

They get right back to where they started. They start making money, and they get overconfident again and they go through it, again. They take the risks and they break the rules and they get their heavy losses and then they have to start yet again.

At some point these people will quit because they can't get it into their heads that the whole thing is about planning and discipline and making money. Unfortunately, so many people go through this cycle and they might even go through it many times.

Here is what I want to say to you... Please, please, please, understand what I have written and shared here and just do Stage 1 and Stage 2.

Plan effectively, practice self-discipline, trust the process, stick to the strategy, and make yourself some money.

Make yourself consistent money, compound your account, and make this into the most fantastic thing you've ever learned.

If you do, it will give you results for the rest of your life.

Make it happen for yourself. You owe it to yourself and your family.

Follow what I've said - plan, practice discipline, make money, and forget those other three things that the stupid people do.

Don't let that be you.

If you are beginning to think, "What will happen if I make just this one tweak?" If you start going to those places, then you need to sit yourself down and give yourself a good talking to. Because if you don't, it will all end in tears and empty pockets!

Please seek help if needed, and make sure you stay a disciplined trader who is making some money.

Summary

Everything in this chapter needs to be very clear for you and you have to understand the importance of these simple truths. Allow my years of experience and teaching to guide you with the simple mindset strategies I've presented in this chapter.

Without the proper mindset, you can have the greatest strategies in the world, and you will still lose money or simply not make money. However with the correct mindset you can have success and true wealth.

PART FOUR

Part Four will show you how to manage your trading income so that you build true wealth over time. It will also give you a guided tour of the principles of compounding. It will show you what can be achieved using what Albert Einstein called 'the eighth wonder of the world.'

Chapter Nineteen - Wealth Management

If you follow through on the steps I have taught you throughout this book, it will be possible to research a solution, take action to model the chosen system and make a regular income from trading. Once you have this source of income, it will be time to start multiplying the results from your activity.

The secret of true wealth is to build up a fund that is large enough for low levels of interest from it to supply all your income needs without having to draw funds down from the capital.

The quickest way to do this is to apply the principles of compounding to your trading and investing practices. Albert Einstein called compound interest the eighth wonder of the world, and rightly so.

I fully understand that you may want cash flow now and you are most likely reading this book because you want to make lots of money from the stock market. But train yourself to move away from quick gratification. Instead, focus on how you can reinvest even minimal amounts of your trading profits to take advantage of the compounding effect because the rewards you will reap from it in a few years will be absolutely massive.

Make the time to think about this and decide whether to spend or not to spend and consider only taking your cash flow to spend on absolute necessities, using the rest to reinvest in your future.

By sticking rigidly to your strategies, you will make consistent profits and then make further profits on those profits; continually building and expanding your wealth.

Although it's always great to spend some of the profits, learning to put some aside will increase your wealth substantially.

Chapter Twenty - Compounding

You will get such joy from moving through this process of reinvesting and compounding. You will be able to see results with each passing month and have the satisfaction that your money is growing.

Eventually you will get to a point where there is so much money coming from your cash flow, that you will effectively get a pay rise every single month. Just think of that!

The growth of your funds will be like a snowball rolling down a hill, picking up more and more snow and getting larger as it rolls down the hill and you won't be able to stop the size from increasing.

You will be making a constant cash flow all of the time, the amount always increasing.

I strongly encourage you to experience the benefits of compounding.

Now that we can visualize the principle of the compound effect, let's look at a conservative trading example so we can examine the numbers.

Non-compounding

$20,000 traded in a strategy that produces just 1.5% return per month (18% per annum) will produce $3,600 per year. If you spend the $3,600 profit, you will get that $3,600 every year and that amount will never increase because you are not compounding. You will always have $20,000 capital and you will always make $3600 per year.

Compounding half of your returns

However, if you took that amount and reinvested half of it every month, you would spend $1,800 per year and invest the other $1,800 per year. This would be reinvesting. Each month, $150 (a twelfth of $1,800) would go into the fund where you began with the original $20,000.

If you did that for ten years, do you know how much you would have in your fund? That original amount would compound to $49,000 over those 10 years.

Now that's pretty amazing in itself, but now that that amount has grown, how much income is it now producing?

The income that would produce at the same 1.5% return per month would now be over $8,000 per annum.

Isn't compounding great?

Compounding all of your returns

That result was achieved by just reinvesting half of the money we are earning from our trading. Now let's see what happens if you reinvested the whole 1.5% per month.

You would now be reinvesting $300 dollars per month (a twelfth of the $3600 you earn each year)

After 10 years, the original $20,000 would be worth over $119,386 and the annual return in year 10 would be $19,533.

Doesn't that sound a whole lot better than what you started with? You started, remember, with $20,000 investment capital and the return on that was $3,600 per year.

You see putting off taking some of your income from trading can be massive to yours and your family's future. I strongly advise using this lesson. Think of every expenditure as an opportunity to create a better future for yourself through compounding. This doesn't mean don't live today. It just means showing some restraint for a few small years so you don't have to show as much in future years!

You see it's not hard to become wealthy over time if you are consistent in your reinvestment strategy

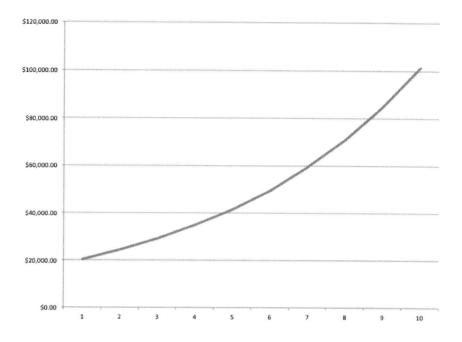

Here is an example of $20,000 compounded over 10 years at a rate of only 1.5% per month.

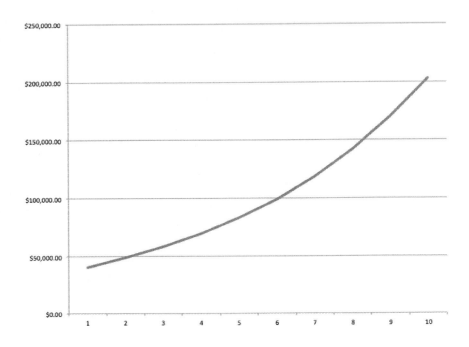

Here is an example of $40,000 dollars compounded over 10 years at a rate of only 1.5% per month.

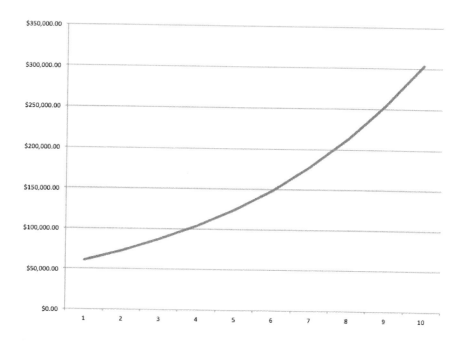

Here is an example of $60,000 dollars compounded over 10 years at a rate of only 1.5% per month.

Compounding consistent income is without doubt where your future ambitions should be.

Building Wealth Over Time

You do not have to be massively wealthy to become a trader. Nor do you need to have $50,000 to invest if you are happy with the element of compounding. You can start from just about anywhere.

If all you want to do is to replace your IRA and save up for retirement, you can see the value of the compounding element alone and know it will build your wealth. You might not actually want any of the money now at all and prefer to reinvest all of it because it just keeps building.

It might be a fund for the future. Perhaps you are in a job now and you would like to quit or retire in ten years' time. Or you are building a college fund for your children. Whatever the reason, it allows you to build wealth over time. That is the power of compounding. When you reinvest stock returns and compound, you can slowly exit your day job.

Compounding is an excellent way to grow your wealth over time and knowing that you are positively working towards a better financial situation brings a certain sense of well-being and peace now. You understand that you don't have to get there overnight.

This is not "get rich quick." This is "get rich, slow and steady."

Think of the tortoise and the hare. Those who are trying to do it overnight have many obstacles come into their way. While those who take calm and steady action eventually reach their goal.

Trader or Investor?

Have you ever noticed that in life people love to place you in a pigeonhole? Everybody does it every day.

He's a Democrat. She's a Republican.

Let me give you two classics from the world of stocks and shares:
He's a Trader.
She's an Investor.

So how are these pigeonholes usually described?

Investor

Most people would regard an investor as someone who adopts a long-term 'buy and hold' strategy. They buy into a fund or series of funds of stocks over a long period of time and do not worry about short-term fluctuation in the market.

Trader

Most people would regard a trader as someone who moves in and out of stocks or funds within a short period of time and is less focused on the long-term future.

Why did I bring these two definitions up? Because I believe that to position yourself in either of the two camps is to do yourself a disservice and lose your focus on what's important.

Your focus, I'm sure, is to build wealth and capital growth over time to support yourself and your loved ones in the future. You can do this using either the investor approach or the trading approach but the ideal in all situations in life is probably to use a mixture of everything that can aid you and that is economical with your time.

The options strategies that I have outlined to you provide you with a mixture of both long-term and short-term money solutions which when combined with compounding will serve you well.

From now on then, no pigeonholing, no labeling!

Build your wealth for the future in only five minutes a day.

PART FIVE

Part Five will show you how to get started and prepare you for your trading journey. Part Five also includes an online resource page that provides you with a trading toolkit of free resources to help you on your journey.

Chapter Twenty-One - Set Yourself Up to Win

Why are some people more successful than others at trading? The answer is simple—because winners set themselves up to win. Successful traders are prepared through the act of great preparation.

Abraham Lincoln said, "Give me six hours to chop down a tree and I will spend the first four sharpening the axe."

This is not a reference to procrastination; it is not about thinking long and hard about the task at hand, like most of us do with big decisions in life. It is about getting down to solid preparation right away and sharpening the axe of preparation.

People who are successful at trading are successful because they learned a specific strategy. They learned how to apply it consistently and they are at a point where they trust their trading process implicitly. They made sure the strategy fitted in with their lifestyle and proved to be achievable. They made the commitment to learn and they followed that up with consistent action every day in order to make their dreams become their reality. It is not hard to be consistent when you want something enough, when you understand what it can give you.

If you are going to be a successful trader, what are the essential things to focus on?

1. They prepare. They understand what is necessary to find the right strategy.
2. They learn from others. They take that important first step.
3. They start. They take rapid action on what they've learned.
4. They continue with consistent action and understand the power of that consistency.

When you do the above four things, you will get the consistent results that successful traders get.

Successful traders plan for the long term and understand the power of compounding. You do not have to make massive returns immediately because the consistent monthly returns of just one or two percent will, over time, amount to great wealth and security when these techniques are applied.

All of my students and I make returns approaching 20% per year. Some of us make even more than that just by applying these principles with focus and determination.

Chapter Twenty-Two – The Gold Star Trading Model

In this chapter I'm going to take you through my *Gold Star Trading Model,* which will show you five structured steps to take you towards getting the perfect trading solution for you.

This is really a summary of how to get started. It isn't about THE best strategy. It isn't about THE best course or program. It is about THE best book. It's an invitation to you to have a good look around and prepare properly rather than plunging headlong into the first strategy that takes your fancy.

We're going to talk about how to set yourself up in trading so you have the very best probability of success. Don't forget Abraham Lincoln and his axe! Preparation is THE key to successful trading and the *Gold Star Trading Model* is all about preparation.

This model has taken me ten years to discover and perfect. Remember, I said that selecting the right approach to trading is what can make trading so straightforward and simple. In sharing this, I am giving you a massive shortcut to begin with right now. So are you ready?

There are five key elements that need to be mastered in order to be a successful trader:

1) Identify the Strategy That Fits with You and Your Lifestyle

Without a strategy that fits in with you and your lifestyle, you have nothing. As soon as you get a working trading strategy that fits in with you and your lifestyle, YOU are on your way to success.

2) Choose Your Broker

In order to be in control of your own trading, you need an online trading platform and there are many to choose from. But remember, while you trade, these people are looking after your hard-earned money. Make sure you find one that is secure so you know your money is protected.

3) Get Reliable Market Information About The Financial Markets

Information is a funny thing. There is a lot of it out there, but for true success you need information that is accurate and independent. You don't want someone's point of view about what is happening in the market. You need accurate and concrete information. Make sure the information you get is reliable.

4) Ongoing and Dedicated Support

There are a number of obstacles that can get in people's way when they begin to trade. The only sure way to eliminate these problems and guarantee success is to get the support of a third party who can mentor you through to your trading success.

5) Strategies for Wealth Management

If you are going to be in charge of your own financial future, then there's more to money than just making it. You will want to know how to take care of, and hold onto, every dollar you make. You will need to know how to best make your money work harder for you in the future.

So now that you have seen an overview of my *Gold Star Trading Model*, I am sure you can see how these five key things will deliver a resilient approach to your trading.

Let's dive even deeper into each one of these elements:

Compatible Strategy (One that Fits You and Your Lifestyle)

If you don't know by now what a trading strategy is, don't worry; it's really quite simple. A strategy is your specific tactics or the method that you stick with in order to win the game. In American football it would be the team's playbook; in soccer or European football it might be your playing formation. Basically, your trading strategy is a way that you agree to upfront on how you are going to play the game.

What are the most important things in selecting a strategy?

It needs to fit in with your time scales and your life.

If your strategy dictates that you sit in front of the computer for three hours each day and you know that you do not have three hours extra in each day, then guess what? You won't be successful at it. That is not the right strategy for you and you will not succeed with that strategy no matter how others do with it.

Your strategy needs to be easy to understand.

I know that you're probably busy—we all have things in our lives continuously going on. Wouldn't it be great if you found a strategy that was quick and easy to learn? Few of us have the time to attend long classes and courses that take months of time before we gain any understanding. And speaking of time, wouldn't it be great to have something that you can learn and implement quickly? I'm sure we'd all agree that we are fed up working 40, 60 or even 80 hours a week to earn our money, so the last thing we want is that our new trading strategy acts as a replacement for our job. Search out the strategy that is going to be quick to learn and quick to execute but brings in income all the same.

The strategy needs to be low risk.

We can never eliminate risk altogether, we know that. Even in our jobs, our income is at risk all of the time. What we want is an approach that is sensible and low risk. In trading, if you are not chasing lottery-winning type results and you are not greedy, then you will do just fine. Your trading will be low risk because you are content with a steady income and making good use of it.

The strategy needs to be results-focused.

Be conscious and aware in thinking about the result you want. Focus on sustained results that deliver more and more over time. Don't allow yourself to get obsessed with the odd quick win. A smaller percentage consistently every month will serve you much better than waiting on that occasional jackpot bonanza that lots of people in the stock market are focused on.

Choose Your Broker

Once we have a working strategy that fits with us and our lifestyle, the next thing we need is an online computer-based platform to trade the markets.

Broker choice based on convenience

There are many brokers around and accessing them online is fantastic. It means you can place your trades instantly over an Internet connection from anywhere in the world.

Broker choice based on cost

Because these trading systems are electronic and don't need people involved to make the transactions happen, it also means the trading cost is very low. Opening a brokerage account is free. Your broker makes money each time you trade, so there are no actual costs upfront to open an account.

Broker choice based on protection

The third and very important thing to consider is who will be storing your money. When you begin to make more money and you build your trading fund, the broker stores your money. In essence, it's much like a bank deposit account. For this reason, you need to check how well your money is protected in the event of any financial failure of your broker.

Read carefully through your broker's terms and conditions. Make sure they protect your money in the case of their failure. As an example, some US brokers are protected in the same way as financial institutions. This means the individual accounts at the broker are protected up to $500,000 by the US government. That is great protection. I reside in the UK where our regular bank accounts are not even protected to £100,000 sterling by the government.

In addition, some of the brokers protect individual accounts up to the same amount by insurance. This is the kind of strong protection you should be looking for. It is out there: so don't settle for anything less.

Reliable Market Information

All trading strategies demand that you gather pricing information from the market about your chosen stock or asset class. This data comes from charting software that allows you to study the price data and other useful information.

There is one key element to the information you get from the market. You need your market information to be independent. Luckily I've got some independent charting software that I can recommend to you which is totally free! At the end of this book is the Trading Toolkit where I will tell you to access this free software.

Ongoing and Dedicated Support

Have you ever read a book, listened to an audio program or taken a course that thoroughly inspired you? As you put the book down, finished listening to the audio, or left the course, you were determined to go home and start taking action right away to make the most of your newfound knowledge.

Me, too.

But then somehow the days and weeks passed by and life got busy. Despite your good intentions, the action never happened and all of that great new information you received was wasted and never came to much of anything.

That kind of experience is not unusual and here's why. Most of us get overwhelmed really quickly when faced with something new. With no one by our side to encourage us, keep us focused and on track, we lose our power to act.

To me, the biggest sin in any learning program is the lack of ongoing support. In trading, ongoing support is doubly important because for most people, the whole concept of trading is outside of their comfort zone. After all, we are brought up to think that we should entrust the task of investing to someone else.

My advice is that you ensure that any trading program you choose provides robust and ongoing support. Most people who provide support do charge for it, so allow for this in your budget. If someone happens to include this in their course or program, be grateful because this will make mastering trading so much quicker and easier.

Your support should include regular opportunities to ask questions and the ability to review all the systems you have learned at regular intervals.

Consistent and reliable support is essential to your success.

Understanding Wealth Management

The final piece of the preparation that I have been outlining in this *Gold Star Trading Model* is Wealth Management. We human beings are very good at thinking our main task in life is to amass more money. Unfortunately we spend so much time thinking about making money that we neglect a very important fact.

Once we make the money we need to have mastery of the skills that are required to hold onto it and grow it.

In Part Four I've already dealt with this subject in detail. At this point in the *Gold Star Trading Model* I just want you to make sure that part of preparation to trade is making sure you have a clear plan for managing your money. It runs through everything from researching your approach into your Trading Plan and then into execution of your money management once you have traded.

Gold Star Trading Model Review

So let's review the *Gold Star Trading Model*:

- Identify the strategy that fits with you and your lifestyle
- Choose your Broker
- Get reliable market information about the financial markets
- Seek dedicated support
- Understand Wealth Management

Follow the whole of the *Gold Star Trading Model* as you prepare to trade and you will give yourself every chance to become wealthy over time. Remember, it is not about getting rich quick. The principles I teach are simple and the preparation doesn't take long, so ensure you take time with the preparation.

It is very easy to get distracted by the next new thing, the next new trading strategy and move from one to the other without mastering anything. Don't be a magpie and chase every new shining penny. If you take your time in preparation and choosing your trading approach, you will save yourself years of struggle.

Chapter Twenty-Three - Your Trading Environment

Create Your Perfect Trading Environment

Once your mind and focus become clear, make sure to keep it that way. It's very easy to get distracted when you're trading. It is also very easy, when something becomes familiar, to overlook something and make a mistake that could cost you money.

Most people who trade from home sit in front of their laptop or their computer. They are in an environment where many things are going on. The telephone might be ringing, the children might be noisy, there might be a knock at the door, a good song might come on the radio and you might want to sing along, a text might appear on your mobile phone, or an email might pop into your inbox. All of these things take you away from the key thing that you're doing right now, which is executing a trading strategy perfectly to make you some cash flow.

How can you help yourself? How can you make sure that you have the very best chance of being a disciplined trader who is focused and executes the strategies perfectly each and every time?

Distractions vs. Focus

You have to be sure you are at the right place at the right time.

I am sure you have heard many times in life that being in the right place at the right time can get you just what you want. There is nothing in trading that can get you into the right place at the right time better than being in the correct environment when you are making a trade.

The right time is when we see the correct trading opportunity and the right place is all about having the right environment at the time that trading opportunity comes along. If you have a spare room in your house, that would be the ideal place. You can set up your trading computer in there and go to that place whenever you need to trade. But I'm sure many of you reading this book don't have a spare room, so let's think about how we can take our current environment at home and improve it at the time that we are going to trade.

The steps I go through apply to many people. Perhaps they won't all apply to you, and perhaps all of the solutions won't work for you, but please do everything you can to implement the tips that will work for you to make sure you have a great environment to trade in.

Make Sure You Are On Your Own

Kids:
- Make sure the kids are in bed
- Make sure the kids are studying
- Make sure the kids are occupied

Other adults in the house:
- Make sure they are sat down too. Find out what their favorite program is and buy them a box set of it. Sit them down in front of an episode before you go to your trading. Normally I wouldn't recommend TV to anybody, but in this case their distraction is your gain!

Pets:
- Make sure they are fed, watered and have been let out
- Make sure they cannot come and disturb you

A Separate Room / Area For Training

- As I said before, you might not have a room that you can dedicate to trading away from everything else in the house. At least make sure that your computer is not in a room where everybody else is going to be when you trade. Make sure that you can shut the door and that you will not be disturbed for the window of time that you need for your trading.

Trading Desk

- Keep your desk clear.

Computer

- Turn off email pop-up windows. You know the ones. You're in the middle of something really important and up pops a little box in the corner of your computer screen telling you that you have just received an email, and being the sociable person you are, you just can't resist going on, reading the email, and finding out who it's from.
- It is good to have your trading plan (we'll get to this shortly) on the wall where you can look at it before trading. If your trading space is mobile, have it on your computer desktop AND remember to look at it!
- It is also good to have a trading checklist on the wall. As above, if you move your trading area to different parts of the house, then make sure you have it handy or on your computer desktop so you can be sure you have covered each step.

Chapter Twenty-Four - The Importance of a Trading Plan

Before you begin trading it is *essential* that you create a Trading Plan.

What is the purpose of a Trading Plan?

Your trading plan outlines how you are going to trade, and it is important to write it down and "set it in stone" so to speak, to make sure you are very clear about it.

Again, this seems simple and you may be thinking, "I'll write it later" or "I know what to do, it's so easy, I don't have to write it down." But I want you to write it down so you have that extra clarity. More so, by writing it down you will have a solid document that says this is how you're going to trade. This is your agreement with yourself. It is how you will operate as a trader.

There are three primary reasons for you to do this;

> 1) You will better understand the importance of your trading plan
> 2) You want to make sure that your trading plan works for you
> 3) You make sure it has the right level of importance in your life

Once again, let me remind you how important the trading plan is just in case you feel this is something that you don't have to bother with and you think you can skip it and it won't have any consequence.

You absolutely need to do this, and here's an example of its importance in the real world. For someone who works on the trading floor in a financial institution, the importance of a plan is paramount. This trader can actually makes huge amounts of money for the financial institution but also could potentially lose huge amounts of money for the financial institution.

To ensure that the trader is aware of this importance, this is what happens on a professional trading floor. Each individual trader has to develop a trading plan based on their skills and their knowledge in trading. They have to write their rules of the game. They must say, "This is how I'm trading," and put that to paper. "This is how I'm going to operate and I'm never going to break these rules. I'm never going to do anything different."

They naturally have a trading floor manager or head: somebody who is in charge of the trading floor.

They both sit down together and they go through this plan. If the plan is acceptable with the trading manager, and both know that the trader can perform the written strategy well, they both sign the document at the bottom. They agree that, "Yes, this is exactly how things are going to operate and it is the only way I, the trader, agree to trade for this financial institution." That is not word for word, but you understand the principle. When they both sign the agreement, that trading strategy is set in stone and that is the only way the trader is allowed to actually trade.

Let me tell you what happens if that trader subsequently does something that isn't on that trading plan.

They will be fired on the spot.

Immediate, instant and permanently. Just like Donald Trump, "You're fired!" and that is the end. No warnings. No nothing.

They are asked to clear their desk, they are promptly escorted out of the financial institution and they no longer have a livelihood, or even favorable references anymore.

The reason that happens to them is different from the way most people get disciplined in a regular job. In a regular corporate job, you may first be sent to human resources or the procedure may be to attend a few special meetings. The procedure normally allows for some room for error and improvement because everyone makes mistakes. Everyone deserves a second chance, right?

Not in trading.

The consequences of breaking the trading plan are very well understood by financial institutions. They know exactly how harmful it is to that individual trader's performance. There is no room for error.

If financial institutions recognize the importance of the plan and also understand the severity of breaking a plan, shouldn't you take a leaf out of their book and treat you plan with the same seriousness?

Having a trading plan and following it will make you more money. It's as simple as that. Make sure you use one.

Chapter Twenty-Five - Your Trading Plan

Initial Planning

Your trading plan should be clear and your guide to successful trading. When writing your plan, set aside at least 30 minutes and really think about this important promise you are making to yourself, and make sure to view it every day before you begin to trade.

This is how you should lay out your trading plan:

Date

Your Mission Statement

What are you looking to achieve with your account?

Example: I am trading to create a solid capital foundation ($xxx,000) that will enable me to generate $xx,000 dollars per month using low risk covered call option writing strategies.

The key message here is *be specific*. Use your 'Reason Why' that we talked about earlier in the book to populate this section of your trading plan.

Your Attitude to Risk

If your mission is aggressive, you may adopt a medium risk.
Here's an example for a cautious investor: I am a cautious and risk-averse investor.

Your Primary Aims

What will dictate your actions and strategies? Do you want to minimize losses and take less risk, e.g. some will be happy losing nine trades out of ten because they know when the one works, it had a win ratio of 20 to 1? Others will take low risk and have low win ratios so they need to be more cautious with each trade.

Here's a low risk example:
> I will protect my capital FIRST.
> I will get consistent monthly results that compound over time to greater capital.

Your Strategies

What strategies will you use?

Example: I will use the *The Cashflow Trader Program*. This strategy involves generating money by selling puts and calls on the SHARE NAME.

Your Trading Rules

You will use this section to list the main steps of your chosen strategy or strategies.

Your Money Management

Examples:
> I will protect the compounding effect of my account at all costs. I will only withdraw essential money from the trading account.
> Money that is essential to pay bills
> Money that reduces debt and improves my credit rating
> Money that pays the mortgage, etc.

Obviously, my hope is that you will start with a low-risk strategy, maybe the options trading strategy that I have been outlining in this book, but no matter how simple or which strategy you ultimately choose, it needs to be written down. You should not do your first trade without your trading plan in place and again, be very clear in writing your aim and your exact strategy.

In my experience, people always start with the best intentions, but soon begin to deviate from the plan. They want to try new things and different things and this is where trouble begins. Remember how a professional trader on Wall Street would be treated if he deviated from his trading plan.

Taking any actions that are not in your trading plan are a deviation and a danger. Understand that you should not deviate, and remind yourself by looking at your trading plan every day. Write it down, be clear on your aims, be clear on your strategies and stick to the plan.

Revising your Trading Plan

Now in the future, will it be okay to revise your trading plan?

Yes, it will, but there is a strategic (and safe) process as to how it should happen: If you do happen to learn other things in the future and you decide you want to operate those extra strategies, that's fine. What you want to do is take yourself away from your trading, sit down and revise your trading plan. Then move away from the old trading plan and go to the new trading plan with your new set of rules.

This takes time and thought. You are completely revising and creating a new trading plan in a calm and controlled environment where you are not being distracted. You can think logically and make a rational decision. This is completely different from just sitting down one day in front of your computer when you've got the trading plan there and saying, "I'm not going to do what's on that trading plan today. I'm going to try something different." That is dangerous and remember, if you were on Wall Street, you'd be sent to the curb in five minutes!

There are reasons for this. Trading can be like gambling for some people and those people can lose control. They lose their heads and often their money, on a moment's decision when they do not follow a plan.

When you are on Wall Street, you know that getting sacked, cleaning your desk out immediately, getting thrown out of the building, never being able to come back, not having a livelihood, is what happens. Imagine the effects if you make such a decision and you make a poor choice in the heat of the moment. It can cost you all of the work you have done up to now, and quite literally, your entire financial security in your future. The results of a moment's non-thinking can be devastating so please, do not deviate from your plan.

Making a decision to revisit or revise your trading plan once every six months, or once a year (like a professional trader would do with his trading manager), and agreeing to the rules for the coming year is absolutely fine.

Now you understand that the purpose of a trading plan is to show you a clearly defined and structured approach to your trading. With it, you will never decide to try something different on a spur of the moment.

Chapter Twenty-Six - Your Trading Toolkit

I have created this section of the book to share with you some of the resources that I personally use in my trading.

One of the things that I am most proud of in my teaching is that everything I show my students to do in trading can be achieved using freely available resources on the Internet. No one has to subscribe to a specific piece of paid software in order to trade powerful consistent option strategies.

I considered adding a complete list of the resources I use in this section, however I am always frustrated when I go to the resource section of a book and see that the various websites no longer exist and the resources are not there. For this reason, I am providing just one link that will take you to the resources I use. As they are centrally located in one place, it allows me to monitor the resources, making sure they stay up to date and that the most current information is available to you.

The Trading Toolkit includes free trading tools, shows you where to find the best virtual trading platform and stock charts. In addition, you will also have access to videos that offer advice on using these tools as well as some free tutorials I teach online.

To take advantage of this, visit

www.the-cashflow-trader.com/bookbonus

Your Secret Weapon to Trust - Virtual Trading

Virtual trading is where you can practice any trading strategy you choose with paper or virtual money.

At the Book Bonus Site given in the previous chapter you will find a link to Options Xpress, who are my current broker, and they have a great virtual trading platform.

The greatest benefit of virtual trading is that you can learn about mistakes without having to pay for them. Learn from mistakes and use the lessons to your advantage.

When you have made all your mistakes and you can see the system you have chosen working time and time again without error, you will have arrived. You will "Trust The Process" and you will have no fear of using real money to trade and invest with.

Chapter Twenty-Seven - Take Control Of Your Own Finances

So, why not take control of your own finances?

It is really not that difficult.

How much money are you going to pay your IFA or your fund manager over the next ten years to look after your money? You do not even know what they are going to do with it. If you took the money you were going to pay them over the next ten years and you invested it in learning trading, how much better off do you think you would be by the time you are 50 or 60 or whatever your target age is?

Educate yourself

You are reading my journey and advice and beginning the preparation of modeling. That is precisely why you have this book in your hands.

You may also want to think about spending a little more than $10-15 on information about your investing future just to make sure you are doing something the correct way. Remember the committed piano player's beliefs in comparison to the uncommitted piano player. Which one took the next step and sought out the mentoring and education needed to be the very best?

If you want to shortcut your own journey and learn from other people's mistakes, they are not going to tell you for free. I share this with you because it is true. Those who forged the new or undiscovered path did so at great personal expense and while they want to make it easier for you, it cost them and they have every right to demand a fair price for showing you the way.

You are on the path already; you have this book, but please do not stop here because there is so much more to learn.

Research and use all the lessons that you learn in this book about how to select the right trading program.

Today versus Tomorrow

Visualizing the future in advance

It is natural for most people to be cautious and only start trading with a small amount of money, but there are ways you can see the future in advance.

When my students start trading, I ask them to consider what they would do with $50,000 in their trading account. I ask them to open a virtual account in addition to their actual cash account and put that $50,000 in the virtual account to see what happens when they trade with a significant fund.

The interesting thing that happens is that they begin to see the effects of utilizing the money today, versus leaving it and compounding towards tomorrow.

When you are ready to begin, why don't you put $50,000 in your virtual trading account and take all the same trades as you are taking with the minor investment you begin trading with in your real account. Watch what happens to that $50,000 over the first year. As you see the numbers grow, use it as a tool to pull you towards your desired outcome.

Watching the virtual account grow is similar to having a massive goal set there in front of you, written down. Each and every day you can see what it is actually going to be like when you've got a lot of money there.

It is very important for you to understand where you can be and to allow that focus to drive you and push you towards those goals.

Life is ongoing and not merely a one-year event. It is very important that you understand where you could be in ten years' time if you start taking some action today. While ten years may seem far away, think back to something that happened ten years ago now.

My oldest is child is eleven and those last ten years have gone by quite rapidly. Ten years ago I did not think it would, but it did. Even though your mind can be tricked into thinking it is a long time away, it really is worth starting now.

Chapter Twenty-Eight - Trading Myth Busters

Isn't Trading Technical?

Understand that this is not going to be technical. If you have a PC or can buy a PC, you can trade online. There isn't anything fancy to learn and it is as easy as writing with a pen and paper. You can literally be up and running within minutes.

Don't I Need A Financial Background To Understand Trading?

Do not worry if you don't have a financial background. This isn't about mathematics; it's about following a few simple instructions in the correct order.

Do you know how to make yourself a bowl of cornflakes?

- Get a bowl out of the cupboard
- Pour in the cereal
- Get milk out of the fridge
- Pour on cereal

If you can follow the instructions I have offered, in the correct sequence, then as simply as getting yourself a bowl of cereal, you can trade.

I don't mean to be flippant, but I do want you to know that this is very easy to learn. The only reason you don't know how yet is because someone hasn't shown you. It's not because trading is beyond you. Anyone can do it, and do it successfully.

It Will Take Too Much Time

If you believe that you don't have the time, there are many brokers around and accessing them online is also simple. It means you can place your trades instantly over an Internet connection from anywhere in the world. When you think about this, it is truly amazing. I can be sitting at a beach bar on vacation and check my trading charts and place a trade in less than five minutes from my telephone. Of course, if you're at the beach bar trading, I recommend drinking water rather than the cocktails they serve – it's not a good idea to trade when you've been drinking!

Because our trading systems are electronic and don't need people involved to make the transaction happen, it also means that the trading cost is very low. Yes, the brokers have to charge money every time you trade–that's how they make their money–but the costs are very low in comparison to the value of the trade itself.

Don't I Need Specialist Software And Doesn't That Cost Money?

The charting software that I use and recommend is free and accessible over the Internet. Many trading courses get you to use software with monthly subscriptions and they use fancy plugins that result in even more monthly costs. I don't believe in doing that. Again, the software I recommend and use is free.

This is why strategy choice and educational choice is so important. Choose the right strategy and the right support and you can reduce the ongoing costs of trading as well as the cost of learning to trade successfully in the first place.

Shouldn't This Be Left To An Expert?

I'm going to let you in on a little secret. Most advisers are people who work in high street financial institutions and profess to know the best way to look after your money. Those who tell you to invest in their products and services, of all those people, most are no different to 95% of the population – they are broke or very near broke.

Most people in our society are three paychecks away from bankruptcy. They stop earning and three months later, after not being able to service their credit, they are over.

If you doubt what I say, the next time your Financial Advisor recommends a fund to you, ask them this question: How many tens of thousands of dollars do you have invested in this product?

I guarantee you that 9 times out of 10 the advisor will tell you "none."

Conclusion - Start Now – Seize The Day

Let me be very clear: no one looks after your money better than you.

Your money is more important to you than it is to anyone else and in my book, that is precisely what makes you the best qualified person to look after it, especially in terms of investing.

Of course you're going to seek the right knowledge to help you and I know that's why you have been reading this book.

Financial Freedom

Now that you know what you have to do, it's a lot easier to be focused and to get started. When you begin trading and you master it, you will have a skill for life that provides a regular additional income stream.

If you are working now, you will have the security of knowing that you have a steady second income. The peace of mind of knowing there is something to fall back on should your job suddenly cease to exist. Better yet, this additional income stream can eventually overtake and replace your income so you never need to work again.

This is a real possibility when you apply the principles of compounding, because in essence, it is as though you are getting a significant pay raise each and every year. Imagine never having to work for someone else again. No boss, just consistent income.

Time Freedom

But the best part of all is the time freedom. You'll be making your money in less time so you can enjoy more of your life and spend more precious time with those you want to be with.

I have shared this knowledge because I want to see more people experience this. I want others to know the pleasure of being self-sufficient, being your own boss and having time freedom to live the way you want to live.

It is my hope that you will implement all that I have shared with you so you too can reap the rewards. Money is not a scarce resource on the planet, you just need to learn how to get it, and I hope I have provided that to you in this book.

However, time IS scarce.

Time is scare for us all. The good news is that we can have a lot more of it if we focus on the money creation tools that don't take much time.

As I said at the beginning of this book, the information I have shared herein used to be shrouded in mystery and out of our reach, but now we can all access these tools using conservative strategies, keeping risk to a minimum and make consistent income every month.

Five minutes per day to get your life back. That is all.

The real question is, do you want your life back?

I challenge you to begin.

About the Author

Jeremy Downing is a successful trader and property investor. He has been trading successfully in financial markets for over a decade.

He has introduced thousands of people to trading over the years whilst working across different trading methods and has created and teaches *The Cashflow Trader Program* and *The Options Trading Master Class*. He also coaches high net worth clients, one on one, in stock options trading. He has taught using his *Triple Success Method,* which combines video tutorials, success coaching and classroom teaching to produce high levels of satisfaction with his students.

Jeremy's experience as a property investor led to his unique approach to trading which stems from his desire to make trading as solid as property investing. Jeremy has spoken on *Applying the Principles of Property Investing to the Stock Market*, *The 5 Biggest Obstacles to Successful Trading and How To Avoid Them* and also regularly speaks on goal setting and planning.

Jeremy's Education Company, *The Successful Trader*, began by teaching his clients how to trade for themselves. In January 2013, *The Successful Trader* released *The Cashflow Trader Program* which teaches individuals from all walks of life how to earn a monthly cash flow from the stock market using stock option strategies. With its low-risk and low-time commitment approach, *The Cashflow Trader Program* provides a simple and effective way to make up to 20% per annum from a small time commitment of just five minutes a day.

Jeremy spends his spare time writing music and as an English Football Association Qualified Coach. He coaches youth in their football skills.

Glossary

Here is a list of some frequently used trading terms.

Calendar (Trading) – A calendar that specifies the opening days and hours of the exchange and also lists significant calendar items that may affect the market you trade in. There are a variety of these on the Internet that have different levels of detail. The calendar we recommend is:

http://www.marketwatch.com/optionscenter/calendar.

Call Option – An option acquired by a buyer or granted by a seller to buy 100 shares of stock at a fixed price within a specific time period.

CBOE – Chicago Board Options Exchange

Commission – A fee that is charged every time you make a trade (by your broker).

Expiration Month – Every option traded has an expiration month that is listed as part of the options details. Always make sure you trade an option with the correct expiration date for the strategy.

Expiration Date – The third Friday of the expiration month is the last trading date for an option. The technical expiration date is the next day, the Saturday. This will be the day when the options clearing house will take action on any trades necessary for that option.

Free Stock Charts – A free Internet charting platform that is suitable for your options trading needs and is the recommended charting software for this course. www.freestockcharts.com

Gross Profit – In terms of options trading this is the premium we collect when we sell our options, before subtracting commission charges.

Intrinsic Value – The element of an options premium that reflects the difference between the stock price and the option strike price.

Net Profit – The money you collect from selling options minus any commissions and fees charged.

Option – The right but not the obligation to buy 100 shares of stock at a specified, fixed price and by a specified date in the future.

Option Contract – You may only buy or sell options contracts. Each contract grants an option over 100 shares. 1 Contract = 100 shares.

Option Premium – The amount of money you collect when you sell an option contract or the amount you pay when you buy one. Quoted as amount per share.

Profit – See **Net Profit** and **Gross Profit**.

Profit Calculation - Profit % = Monthly ROI/Invested Capital x 100.

Put Option – An option acquired by a buyer or granted by a seller to sell 100 shares of stock at a fixed price within a specific time period.

Revenue – The income you generate from your trading activity.

ROI – Return on Investment. This is usually shown as a percentage of your capital investment. ROI is calculated by dividing your net profit by the original capital investment and multiplying by 100.

Share – A unit of ownership that represents an equal proportion of a company's capital.

Stock – A stock (also known as an equity or a share) is a portion of the ownership of a corporation. A share in a corporation gives the owner of the stock a stake in the company and its profits. If a corporation has issued 100 stocks in total, then each stock represents a 1% ownership in the company.

Strike Price – The price written into an option contract at which the option is exercisable.

Time Value – The portion of the options premium that reflects the time left to expiration. This decreases the nearer the expiration date becomes.

Virtual Trading – A facility in a trading account that allows the use of virtual funds to assist in learning the trading process and getting to grips with the mechanics of the trading process.

Printed in Great Britain
by Amazon